TEACHING WHEN THE WORLD IS ON FIRE

Also by Lisa Delpit

Other People's Children: Cultural Conflict in the Classroom

"Multiplication Is for White People":
Raising Expectations for Other People's Children

Also edited by Lisa Delpit

The Skin That We Speak:
Thoughts on Language and Culture in the Classroom
(with Joanne Kilgour Dowdy)

TEACHING WHEN THE WORLD IS ON FIRE

*Authentic Classroom Advice,
from Climate Justice to Black Lives Matter*

EDITED BY

LISA DELPIT

NEW YORK
LONDON

© 2019 for the compilation by The New Press
Introduction © 2019 by Lisa Delpit
All rights reserved.
No part of this book may be reproduced, in any form,
without written permission from the publisher.

Requests for permission to reproduce selections from this book should
be made through our website: https://thenewpress.com/contact.

First published in the United States by The New Press, New York, 2019
This paperback edition published by The New Press, 2021
Distributed by Two Rivers Distribution

ISBN 978-1-62097-665-4 (pb)
ISBN 978-1-62097-431-5 (hc)
ISBN 978-1-62097-432-2 (ebook)
Library of Congress Control Number: 2019911433

The New Press publishes books that promote and enrich public discussion and
understanding of the issues vital to our democracy and to a more equitable world.
These books are made possible by the enthusiasm of our readers; the support
of a committed group of donors, large and small; the collaboration of our many
partners in the independent media and the not-for-profit sector; booksellers, who
often hand-sell New Press books; librarians; and above all by our authors.

www.thenewpress.com

Composition by dix!
This book was set in Janson Text and Gill Sans

Printed in the United States of America

To Adelaide Sanford, Septima Clark, Asa Hilliard, Gloria Hebert, Edmae Delpit Butler, and all the other phenomenal educators upon whose shoulders I stand.

And to Patricia Lesesne, Makeesha Coleman, Fernanda Pineda, Charity Parsons, the Urban Teacher Leaders at Southern University, my former students from throughout the country, and all the other young, brilliant educators who have given me the honor and privilege of sharing their teaching journeys. I humbly watch as they set new kinds of fires and change the world.

Contents

Introduction

Lisa Delpit

I REMEMBER SIXTH GRADE. I REMEMBER SITTING IN FRONT OF THE FAMILY television, mesmerized and terrified by the newscasts showing Bull Connor's snarling police dogs attacking young black teenagers, and snarling white policemen simultaneously assaulting them with clubs and powerful fire hoses. I remember how afraid I was when my older sister participated in civil rights protests with her Southern University classmates. I remember adults' fury, frustration, and tears when we heard about four little girls murdered by a bomb while they were in church in Birmingham. I remember how neighborhood rumors periodically spread through the children's grapevine that the KKK would be riding through our community. I remember the day that JFK was shot and the stunned horror that followed in the event's wake. In the mornings, as I combed my hair in my mother's room to prepare for school, I remember watching long lists of names of young men who had been killed in the Vietnam War scroll on the *Today Show*. I remember talk about the Cold War, and the drills in school where we huddled under our desks with our hands over our heads to "protect" ourselves from a nuclear attack. Early in that school year, I remember spending hours in church with other students at my small all-black Catholic school to "rosary-away" the Cuban missile crisis. (Apparently it worked!)

Yes, 1963–64, my sixth-grade year, was tough for me and for all my age mates. The next few years were pretty tough as well, as the fight for civil rights escalated, the Vietnam War intensified, and the Cold War heightened. It was a difficult time to be a child.

And yet, somehow the world feels more frightening now—for children and adults. In the 1960s, there were certainly right-wing politicians, with their only slightly veiled appeals for violence, focused on maintaining segregation and depriving people of color of their citizenship rights. There were organized and unorganized thugs who beat, battered, and killed African Americans who stood up for those rights. Children were afraid for themselves and for their loved ones.

But at the same time, the federal government at least gave lip service—and occasionally support—to the battles waged by its darker citizens. Our leaders could make appeals to the White House to shame the administration into addressing blatant injustices. Citizens of all colors shared a moral outrage that made those who beat young civil rights demonstrators, those who prevented eighty-year-olds from registering to vote, those who threw eggs at school buses and snarled invectives at school children seem barely human.

There was a sense that for all the horror, all the fear, all the injustice, there was always *someone* higher up watching with disapproval: there were allies who wanted to help right indescribable wrongs; there were those who would denounce hatred and its repercussions; there were those who would physically protect the attacked. There were those who knew better.

Today, our children can have no reassurance that the nation has a moral high ground. Rather, all morality from the top has sunk beneath the putrid waters of racism, misogyny, homophobia, xenophobia, irrationality, and despotic bluster. What does it mean to children who not only can see no salvation from on-high, but who find themselves victimized by their highest leaders and the policies they enact? What does it mean when their fellow countrymen join in the victimization with no censure from the highest office of the land? And how are teachers to deal in their classrooms with this current political climate?

This book attempts to answer such questions through an array of responses from classroom teachers, administrators, education professors, and others, reminding today's teachers of their guiding principles and offering constructive, hands-on advice for navigating our nation's choppy waters. A first section on politics opens with a masterful ode to teaching when the world is on fire, in which veteran educator William Ayers urges teachers to post on our bathroom mirrors a list of our reasons for entering the teaching profession, to be reminded daily of our ideals, and to affirm that every student is a three-dimensional being of incalculable value. Justin Christensen, who teaches AP Government in San Francisco, documents five concrete ways to engage students in discussions about Donald Trump without "taking sides." Michigan principal Julia Putnam shows us what restorative justice looks like in a school setting. Education researcher and author Mica Pollock illuminates the role of "preventive speech" in the classroom, offering strategies for combatting hate, and speaking of the critical role for educators in teaching young people to engage across perspectives. Finally, H. Richard Milner IV, professor and editor-in-chief of *Urban Education*, provides concrete tips for respectfully engaging students in difficult conversations.

While the Cold War fear of nuclear attack was real when I was in sixth grade, the danger of deadly violence is even more imminent to today's students. Young people fear losing their lives from school gun violence in a very real way. I was recently in a kindergarten class when an "active shooter" alert was called over the loudspeaker. The teacher locked all the doors, the children huddled in the coat closet with their hands covering their heads, while the teacher issued fierce whispered warnings to be silent. The teacher and children were clearly rattled, with one ending up in tears. It turned out to be a drill, but it reminded me that these drills were considerably more likely to be harbingers of actual events than my sixth-grade drills.

Young people have been engaging in demonstrations and other activism for gun control, but they have been met with official policies that thwart them at every turn. The president's promise of a school safety commission fell flat. The commission's report, in the wake of the 2018 shooting at Marjory Stoneman Douglas High School that killed seventeen people, barely addressed guns, and declined to recommend raising the minimum age for firearm purchases—something student activists and other gun control advocates called for after the Parkland tragedy.

Instead, the Federal Commission on School Safety, led by Secretary of Education Betsy DeVos, took aim at an Obama-era policy designed to curtail the steep racial disparities in school suspensions and expulsions against black and brown students. According to civil rights data at the time the Obama guidance policy was issued, African American students were more than three times as likely as white students to be expelled or suspended. (More than half of the students involved in school-related arrests were Hispanic or African American.)

There is little relationship between the curtailing of disciplinary actions targeting black and brown students and school gun violence, since the vast majority of school shooters are white. Still, the report declared that the Obama policy has had a "chilling effect on school discipline."[1] The report went on to say,

> The Commission is deeply troubled that the [Obama 2014 Rethink Discipline] Guidance, while well-intentioned, may have paradoxically contributed to making schools less safe.[2]

Once more, the current political leadership has pushed for policies that not only fail to provide shelter in schools for any of America's children, but actually target black and brown children in the very institutions that once upon a time promised a sense of safety.

Keeping children safe must be a key priority for any school. In the section "Safety Matters," veteran education expert Pedro A. Noguera talks about the importance of creating trust between teachers and students as a strategy for heading off the growing threat of gun violence in school settings. Jeff Collier, a Texas teacher who is also a PhD candidate, gains new insight into the impact of difficult life circumstances on students' ability to focus in school when he loses his own home to Hurricane Harvey. fredrick scott salyers, an African American teacher in Brooklyn, New York, shares his strategies for helping the African American boys in his class contend with the racism and risk they face, including from law enforcement, on a daily basis. Vermont principal T. Elijah Hawkes describes a restorative justice process implemented at his school to try to address racially biased disciplinary rules. And educator Carla Shalaby offers a tale of a kindergartener giving his teacher a lesson in "being human together" in school.

When I was in sixth grade, school was a safe place for us. Before black students began to desegregate formerly all-white schools, the black school was a central institution in black communities. It was part of our community. The African American teachers knew and socialized with our African American parents outside of school. In our segregated community, we saw teachers in church, in the grocery store, and at community functions. The teachers shared our fears, they shared our parents' hopes for us, they believed that being black was no excuse for not achieving—after all, students and teachers shared ethnicity. They let us know their expectations for excellence and outstanding behavior. The teachers and the school, along with our parents and the larger community, were our defense against a hostile world. Despite the craziness, they were our shelter.

Today, people of African descent continue to exist in the crosshairs of this country's racist history. The Black Lives Matter campaign and other justice-related research efforts have helped bring attention to the many deaths of unarmed black victims at the hands of police, the disproportionate arrest and convictions of young black people as compared to young white people, the disproportionate numbers of black student suspension and expulsions, the poor health outcomes for black communities and many more injustices. This has all had its consequences in the entire community, as even those who are not the direct recipients of unjust actions suffer deleterious repercussions. Dr. Naa Oyo Kwate, a psychologist and professor of Africana Studies at Rutgers, reports on research recently conducted, "So much of what people contend with is not just their individual experience, but also their family and friends and broader society with the police killings."[3]

A school principal I work with in Baltimore told me that since the widely publicized death of twenty-five-year-old Freddie Gray at the hands of police in 2015, and the subsequent acquittal of all six police officers involved, both the children in her school and members of the larger community have been on edge, quick to anger, and quick to start an altercation. She said the students have also exhibited increased symptoms of depression and other emotional and physical health challenges. What happens to one of us can affect us all.

Black Americans have long recognized our role in this country as the proverbial canaries in the coal mine. Whatever issues we are suffering through will eventually make their way to larger segments of society. More and more citizens are now becoming victims of despicable attitudes and destructive national policies. Yet schools struggle with ways to provide the shelter all students need.

In the section "Race Matters," the dean of students at a high school in Harlem, Jamilah Pitts, implores teachers of all disciplines to find ways to open meaningful conversations about race and racial violence in our society, noting that it is far preferable for teachers of all races to express their own confusion and vulnerability to students than to say nothing at all. Bestselling author Christopher Emdin writes about the unique role of black male teachers in the current climate, and specific ways they can empower their students through what Emdin calls Reality Pedagogy. Education professor Wayne Au and Seattle teacher Jesse Hagopian describe an amazing, city-wide Black Lives Matter event in Seattle schools, spearheaded by a local elementary school. Sarah Ishmael and Jonathan Tunstall take inspiration from James Baldwin in seeking to develop age-appropriate curricula around race and racism to douse the flames that many of their African American students seem to be engulfed in. Allyson Criner Brown, who specializes in parent engagement, shares valuable insight about listening to and engaging black parents, and Natalie Labossiere, an African American high school teacher in Oregon, writes about the special challenges facing black teachers and black students in primarily white, suburban schools. Thoughtfully wrapping up this section is Crystal T. Laura, an education professor in Chicago, who makes an impassioned plea for teachers to actively disrupt the school-to-prison pipeline for black boys.

LGBTQ students also experience a lack of safety in school because of a fundamental aspect of their human identities. As if bullying weren't already a problem, the current administration appears poised to put forth policies that erase an entire category of students—those who identify as transgender—and any protection of their rights that accrue to other citizens. According to Eric Green, Katie Benner, and Robert Pear of the *New York Times*, the current administration's Department of Health and Human Services is considering an interpretation of Title IX, the federal civil rights law that bans sex discrimination in federally funded schools, that "would define sex as either male or female, unchangeable, and determined by the genitals that a person is born with." (This would defy the scientific and medical evidence embraced by respected authorities like the American Medical Association and the American Psychiatric Association and remove any rights that transgender students have to appeal any biased treatment they receive.)[4]

With a vulgar and sexist president in the oval office and the #MeToo movement sweeping the country, teachers and administrators today must find ways to address issues of gender, sexuality, and sexism within schools and classrooms. Camila Arze Torres Goitia, a high school teacher from Portland, Oregon, describes a truly inspiring, student-led protest against sexual harassment at her school, resulting in heightened awareness and new policies. Dale Weiss, a second grade teacher, chronicles devising a gender-sensitive curriculum unit in conjunction with a gender nonconforming second grader. And Hazel Edwards, a young trans activist in Philadelphia, describes her work helping educators understand and accommodate trans students—including offering a moving lesson to teachers whose lack of understanding had caused her to drop out years earlier.

Young people today also fear for their future prospects as earth dwellers. Climate change, a significant danger for the future to citizens of the world, has touched many students and their teachers as they study and act to encourage societal awareness and change around the issue. Rather than lend support to their work, the national leadership expresses disdain toward their efforts. The president recently dismissed a landmark report compiled by thirteen agencies of his own federal government that detailed how damage from global warming is intensifying throughout the country, saying he and others like himself have "very high levels of intelligence" and thus are not among the "believers" who see climate change as a pressing problem. But the unequivocal findings that detail how climate change poses severe threats to the country's health, infrastructure, and natural resources are at odds with the current administration's rollback of environmental regulations and absence of any climate action policy.[5] Once again, the children and their futures are compromised.

With climate deniers in control of parts of the government and "climate change" banned from government websites, the question of how to engage with students around global warming looms large for teachers in our nation's schools. Journalist Amy Harmon captures the dilemma in an essay about a science teacher in rural Ohio, who must contend with students whose parents don't endorse the science of climate change. And Bill Bigelow, a veteran social studies teacher and editor of *Rethinking Schools*, recounts the fight in Portland, Oregon, schools to include a comprehensive treatment of our climate crisis and the actions people are taking to address it.

The national climate of nastiness emanating from the country's top political office against those who are least able to defend themselves is reflected in schools and in the policies affecting them. Despite the wishes of many teachers, schools no longer provide the shelter I experienced those many years ago. In 2016, in the days following the presidential election, the Southern Poverty Law Center surveyed ten thousand educators nationwide. According to respondents, students in minority communities were experiencing heightened anxiety and fear for themselves and their families. Educators also reported a sharp uptick in verbal harassment, including the use of racial slurs and hateful language directed at minority students, and prominent displays of swastikas, Nazi salutes, and Confederate flags. According to the educators, these behaviors skyrocketed later in the spring in majority-white schools where white students targeted immigrants, Muslims, girls, LGBTQ students, disabled kids, and Clinton supporters with hateful and biased language. Many educators reported that since the election, what they have witnessed in the schools where they work is, in the words of one teacher, "an unleashing of a spirit of hatred" they had not seen before.[6]

In 2018 the Human Rights Campaign presented the results of its national post-election survey of a diverse group of fifty thousand youth, ages thirteen to eighteen: 70 percent of respondents had witnessed bullying, and of those, 79 percent identified the incidents as related to the campaign and aftermath of the election. In their words, "The bullying effects of the Trump presidency—dubbed the Trump effect—are devastating, particularly when it comes to bullying of minority groups, especially those who are easily identifiable and/or who are singled out by the President's statements."[7]

The consequences of bullying are widespread. As we continue to discover our inherent connectedness, we learn that bullying impacts both the students who are bullied and those who observe the bullying but do nothing about it. Bullied children experience lowered academic achievement, increased health problems, stress, anxiety, and poor concentration. Passive bystanders also suffer as they frequently feel protracted shame for their inaction in the face of injustices committed against their friends and classmates.[8]

School bullying aside, federal immigration enforcement policies and practices have wreaked havoc on any sense of safety many students may have felt in school. Researchers at the Civil Rights Project at UCLA analyzed survey data from 3,500 educators from more than 730 schools across twenty-four districts and twelve states.[9] Many hundreds of respondents reported that immigrant students were terrified that family, friends, and sometimes themselves would be picked up by Immigration and Customs Enforcement. One of the most prevalent and distressing consequences of increased immigration enforcement is the drop in school attendance. Students are afraid to go to school because they worry that a loved one won't be there when they return.

Even when they were in school, it was very difficult for these students to learn and for teachers to teach in this environment. Ninety percent of administrators reported emotional and behavioral problems among immigrant students. Two-thirds of respondents also reported that the fear and concern for classmates was even affecting the education of those students who were not targeted by immigration policies. Many educators reported that when students' family members were deported, the entire school was aware of the situation. This exacerbated fears that other students had about their own situations or those of their friends. Some respondents also reported that in some students' families, one or both parents had been deported or fired due to their immigration status, and there was not enough money for food or other basic needs.

With nationalism, white supremacy, and bigotry on the rise, teachers are finding creative ways to engage their students in resistance. Carolina Drake, a teacher at a progressive New York school with a history of social activism, describes a hands-on curriculum for middle schoolers that includes simulated immigration hearings and trips to Washington to lobby members of Congress. San Francisco English teacher Noah Cho writes about the importance of devising a reading list that allows students of color, LGBTQ+ students, and "students at other intersections" to see themselves in what they read. First- and second-grade teacher Cami Touloukian recounts the amazing, age-appropriate curriculum she and her co-teacher devised for teaching young children in Portland, Oregon, empathy for Syrian war refugees. James Loewen, the bestselling author of *Lies My Teacher Told Me*, reminds teachers to use the world around them, including historical monuments and markers, to teach about our country, noting that these artifacts say as much about the era in which they were erected as they do about the era they commemorate. Finally, Deborah Almontaser, the former principal of the Kahlil Gibran International Academy in Brooklyn, New York, sheds light on how schools can be transformed into safe, welcoming, and nurturing places for Muslim students. And the section concludes with a reading list of books about immigration for young people.

———

Our children are in trouble, and we want to save them; we want to provide them with shelter. But given the larger societal chaos, what can we do? Just as I did when I was in elementary school, I continue to put my faith in teachers. The teachers of my youth, though themselves confined by systematic oppression, gave us students a sense of security in an unsafe world, and inspired dreams that we otherwise could not imagine for ourselves.

Today's teachers are most often undervalued, underpaid, and underestimated, but they, like those strong, persistent black teachers of the past, can make the biggest difference for children in schools that offer no safe haven. This book is both an appeal and a summons for teachers. It is not a manual on how to change schools, but rather provides encouragement and motivation, and most of all, inspiration at a time of growing division, incivility, hate, and violence, for transforming children's lives in sixth—and every other—grade.

Notes

1. Katy Reilly, "Trump's School Safety Commission Is Targeting Obama Anti-Discrimination Rules and Not Guns," *Time*, December 18, 2018, 1–4.

2. Reilly, *Time*, 1–4.

3. Sarah Zhang, "The Physical Damage Racism Inflicts on Your Brain and Body," *Wired*, 3–9 (July 12, 2016, 7:00am), wired.com/2016/07/physical-damage-racism-inflicts-brain-body.

4. German Lopez, "The Trump Administration's Latest Anti-transgender Action, Explained," VOX (October 22, 2018, 11:40am EDT), VOX.com/policy-and-politics/2018110/22/18007978/trump-administration-lgbtq-transgender-discrimination-civil-rights.

5. Josh Dawsey, Brady Dennis, Philip Rucker and Chris Mooney, *Washington Post*, "Trump on Climate Change Evidence: "People like myself, we have very high levels of intelligence but we're not necessarily such believers" (November 28, 2018).

6. Nicki Lisa Cole, "Understanding the Two-Part Trump Effect on America's Schools: Increased Hate and Bias and Fear and Anxiety," *ThoughtCo*, 2–5 (Updated April 16, 2018), thoughtco.com/trump-affect-on-american-education-system-4118208?print.

7. Rosemary K.M. Sword and Philip Zimbardo, "The Trump Effect: An Update: The Toxicity Is Spreading," *Psychology Today*, 1–3 (January 30, 2018), psychologytoday.com/blog/the-time-cure/201801/the-trump-effect?eml.

8. Sword & Zimbardo, "The Trump Effect," 1–3.

9. Patricia Gandara and Jongyeon (Joy) Ee, "U.S. Immigration Enforcement Policy and Its Impact on Teaching and Learning in the Nation's Schools," The Civil Rights Project, UCLA. Paper presented at a forum, "The Impact of Immigration Enforcement Policies on Teaching and Learning in America's Public Schools," in Washington, DC, on February 28, 2018.

TEACHING WHEN THE
WORLD IS ON FIRE

Politics
Matters

I Shall Create!
Teaching Toward Freedom

William Ayers

Bill Ayers is the author of the acclaimed and controversial memoir Fugitive
Days *and many books on education, including* To Teach, Teaching
Toward Freedom, *and* A Kind and Just Parent. *He lives in Chicago.*

"I SHALL CREATE!" A JUVENILE DELINQUENT CRIES OUT IN GWENDOLYN
Brooks's poem, "Boy Breaking Glass," and the words, coming from
the mouth of this imagined "bad boy," land with particular power and
poignancy. "If not a note, a hole," he continues, "If not an overture, a
desecration." No matter what you've been told, Brooks cautions, and
no matter what the pundits and talking heads have insistently pro-
fessed, never doubt for a moment the urgent intent of even the most
marginalized and outcast youth among us: *I shall create.*

And how shall we—teachers, parents, community members—
answer that heartfelt cry, that elemental human aspiration? How shall
we respond to the dreams of youth? How can we see them through the
blizzard of stereotypes that engulf them, and how will we hear their
authentic voices above the steady roar of commentary about them?

We begin by thinking clearly about what teaching is at its best,
what teaching can be or might still become, and what, at its heart,
calls us to teach. No one goes into teaching saying, "I'm so excited to
get into my own classroom where I can sort children into winners and
losers," or, "All my life I've dreamt of prepping youth day after day to

take the high stakes standardized tests," or, "I've worked out an amazing classroom management scheme, and I can't wait to see how well I can control and disciple the little bastards." No teacher thinks like that. As my brother, a legendary California high-school teacher, often said, "I may be an agent of the system or of the state for several hours a day, but I'm a free agent the rest of the time, and I squeeze every drop of life and light out of each moment of freedom—that's where I'm the teacher I truly want to be." We may perform duties not of our choosing, but we're drawn to teaching from a higher place.

What motivates some is a sense of love for children or youth, or perhaps the positive feelings generated when we're in the adventurous company of the young. For others it's a passionate engagement with the world or some part of the world—music or math, say, African American history or poetry, geometry or geography—that invites us to share that love with young people. Others cherish a deep sense that education can change the direction of history and society, or perhaps, more modestly, change the people who will change our communities in promising ways. We come to teaching hoping to make a difference—in children's lives and in the larger world. All of this frames teaching as ethical and intellectual work, something that requires a thoughtful and caring person in order to be done well.

The intellectual and ethical work of teaching can be hard to see in some places—schools that, inadvertently or not, crush souls and break bodies. Not at every turn or in every moment, perhaps, and not all of them all the time, but too many schools, day in and day out, are organized to smash curiosity, impede imagination, shatter self-respect, and deflate the dreams of youth. They reward obedience and compliance while punishing creativity and courage, initiative and ingenuity. This is the brutal masquerade called school offered to the descendants of formerly enslaved human beings, First Nations peoples, and immigrants from colonized communities. For these mostly Black and Brown and poor kids, the classroom marches under the gauzy banner of enlightenment and democracy, empowerment and progress, while operating relentlessly to reproduce and police the hierarchies of winners and losers along predictable lines of race and class. These American schools have inequity and congealed violence baked into their DNA.

Entering our contested classrooms—that space where the eternal conflict between the ideal of teaching and the reality of institutionalized schooling lives—we must think more deeply about our first principles, the tools we carry inside us into teaching every day. The friction is timeless and abiding, and today the contradictions between the ideal and the material are stark: an almost pathological obsession with student results on high-stakes standardized tests; the reduction of education to a single metric; the near-total disregard in the halls of power for the experiences and collective wisdom of classroom teachers; the systematic dismantling of the public space in favor of private management and private profit.

This is galling for those of us who understand learning to be expansive, dynamic, and idiosyncratic, and who believe that an excellent education is the natural right of every child. And so while we note that we may not have as much control as we'd like concerning the contexts within which we work, we surely have more control than we sometimes recognize or exercise regarding our core values, and choosing how we might live out those values in the dailiness of classroom life. Let's access those values. You begin by asking yourself how you intend to live your teaching life in a way that doesn't make a mockery of your teaching values: name as clearly as possible your commitments, spell them out so that you have a handy list to post on the bathroom mirror, a list to consult each morning as you prepare to dive once more into the everyday classroom contradictions.

I'll share my short list here, and maybe a few of these points are already on your list, or maybe a couple will find a place there now. But the important thing is to think deeply, reflect fully, and make your own list. Do it. Post it. Knowing we will all fall short of our ideals in the rough and tumble of real classroom life is no cause for despair or procrastination, and no reason not to posit the ideals you're reaching for—we can try to end each day critical of every failure and shortcoming, and get up the next morning with our minds set on freedom, ready to go at it again, and this time do a bit better.

I'll elaborate below, but here are four commitments that I see, meet, and affirm each day on my way to my classroom, my concise reminders to myself, my personal looking-glass list:

- Every student who comes through the classroom door is a three-dimensional human being like myself, and a person of infinite and incalculable value, someone to be treated with awe and respect, humility and patience.
- Today and every day (and in a zillion ways) we're learning to live together—the environment we strive to create is characterized by honesty, dialogue, critical questioning, fairness, and recognition, not monologue, management, control, or punishment.
- Wherever racism resides, we resist.
- In everything we undertake we foreground the arts of liberty—imagination and creativity, initiative and courage, compassion, ingenuity, and enterprise—as we work to expand the agency of students, and generate transformative possibilities for all of us.

Each Student Is of Incalculable Value

Where do we come from? What are we? Where are we going? What are the circumstances of our lives, and how might they be otherwise?

Each student is a three-dimensional creature, a singular character who will walk the earth but once, forging a twisty, one-of-a-kind track across the landscape. We are each the one-of-one—entirely unique and uniquely capable. To treat anyone like a thing, to attempt to own or exploit or oppress another, to objectify anyone or even to attach a label to any human being is to commit a first-order moral mistake. I reject the idea that students can be known by their statistical profiles—age, gender, race, ethnicity, zip code—and support the refusal of young people to be branded or to submit to a sort-and-punish regime in school.

There's another truth that lies side-by-side and in contradiction with that one: each of us is but one of the many, a human being like all others—we share the experience of being born/thrust into a going-world, each of us a being who imagines and creates, suffers, experiences joy and sorrow, and whose life, long or short, will end in the middle of things. We are entirely unique in one way, and completely common in another—a living contradiction in the classroom and everywhere else, a creative tension to hold on to and learn from. And since teaching is always relational, we interact with the group, and we attend to each distinct individual.

Education for free people is powered by that precious and fragile ideal: every human being is of infinite and incalculable value, each a work-in-progress and a force-in-motion, a unique intellectual, emotional, physical, spiritual, moral, and creative agent, each endowed with reason and conscience, each deserving a dedicated place in a community of solidarity as well as a vital sense of brotherhood and sisterhood, recognition and respect. This means that the fullest development of each individual—given the tremendous range of ability and the delicious stew of race, ethnicity, points of origin, and backgrounds—is the necessary condition for the full development of the entire community, and, conversely, that the fullest development of all is essential for the full development of each.

To be ruled is to be spied upon and summed up, inspected, regulated, and indoctrinated, registered and admonished, corrected and measured, tested and ranked—with all the inherent structural violence packed into those arrangements—while to be free is to throw off that entire system, to reject its hold over our minds as well as its power in the world. Because our minds are set on freedom, our first and fundamental task is to teach free people to be free.

And even here, let's keep the tension between the broader community and each particular person in the front of our minds. "Freedom Now!" was the galvanizing cry of the Black Freedom Movement fifty years ago, and while individual democratic rights were a part of it— the right to movement, the right to eat and sit and drink water wherever one wished—the overall demand was for freedom as a people, for liberation as a community, for a complete break from systemic oppression. People were demanding the right to live and to be fully realized, to develop agency and participatory power, both individually and collectively.

The relationship between education and freedom is deep, intrinsic, and profound—each is concerned with the fullest expression of human development. To the extent that people reflect upon their lives and become more conscious of themselves as actors in the world, conscious, too, of the vast range of alternatives that can be imagined and expressed in any given situation, capable of joining in community and asserting themselves as subjects in history, constructors of the human world, they recreate themselves as free human beings.

Learning to Live Together

This is where the reality of being the one-of-one and being one of the many comes to life in practice. We don't have a rule book or a set of potential crimes and punishments, but we do have an over-arching ethic: respect yourself and respect one another; respect the world and respect the work. Opportunities for teachable moments erupt every day—conflict and resolution—and those can become the unrehearsed yet finest moments of authentic learning and deeper understanding.

Teachers can create classrooms where students with a range of backgrounds, perspectives, experiences, and beliefs can learn to live with and learn from one another. A pedagogy of dialogue—beginning with a question, and then asking the next question, and then the next—is the basic teaching gesture in and for a free and democratic society. Learning the fine art of speaking with the possibility of being heard, and listening with the possibility of being changed, is a prac-tical contribution to finding one's way in a wildly diverse democracy.

We try to tell the truth—the raw and unvarnished, difficult and often unwelcome, sometimes subversive and risky, but also absolutely necessary truth—and work toward mutual understanding. Telling the truth is not wielding dogma like a weapon, nor is it living in a rela-tivistic fantasyland. If we don't try to tell the truth we're trapped in a bughouse, and bedlam surrounds us; if we don't tell the truth we can't develop effective strategies for overcoming obstacles and resist-ing harm—so I'll try to tell the truth to my students as I understand it, and we can struggle together toward deeper truths.

Let's practice some truth-telling—here, for example, is a truth to share with students: we'll spend too much time preparing for high-stakes standardized tests, and yet the truth is that the testing regime is a massive fraud. Corporations profit from it, and that surely says something about why we're enthralled with it, but it's got nothing to do with learning— it's lazy and it's wrong. The fraud is further revealed in a principle borrowed from economics (Goodhart's law), and a similar insight from physics (Heisenberg's uncertainty principle) that illuminates a queer but clever reality: "A performance metric only works as a performance metric if you don't use it as a performance metric." Or: "When a measure becomes a target, it ceases to be a good measure." What that means is that if you want to build a good high school, and you announce, say, that 100 percent college attendance is the preferred indicator, every effort will bend toward that goal, and it might even be achieved—and the school could still be terrible. The target became the goal, and the larger universe remained untouched. We can work to devise strategies and tactics that will resist and upend the toxic impacts of the testing madness on you and your classmates.

One more truth-telling practice, especially for those of us teaching in urban (and, with some variations, other) schools: you've likely come to teaching with hope and the best of intentions, but you should know that the system you'll be joining hates Black and Brown and poor kids—it sounds harsh and unyielding and extreme, but try not to recoil or turn away. I have factual evidence that the system is organized to miseducate these children, and it includes the shameful lack of resources, enforced racial segregation, the dumbed-down and Eurocentric curriculum accompanied by a stifling top-down pedagogy, and arcane rules and routines that result predictably in social shaming and widespread exclusions. We're all asked to participate mindlessly in that nasty work without raising our voices in opposition, but we'll try to build our capacities to tell the truth about that, and to be heard.

The dominant American narrative that glibly labels the Black community as primarily pathological, and Black children and youth as nothing but a collection of pitiable or dangerous deficits, is not true— full stop. We disavow the dismal American habit that blames both poverty and racism on the imagined misbehaviors of poor and Black people. We seek the generative and ever hopeful lessons of radical love and expansive empathy. White people can work to become useful allies and effective organizers, although "ally" isn't quite the right word here because it gestures too easily toward charity as an adequate intervention against racism, white or male supremacy. It's not. We all need to become agents of change, solidarity, and transformation—not a squad of missionaries on a campaign of uplift—if we're to dismantle the racial hierarchy and create the conditions for everyone to get free—not patronizing sentiments but a commitment to equity, justice, recognition, humanization, and emancipation.

Resist Racism

The word "racism" in American vernacular has multiple meanings: in popular usage it mainly means bigotry, often manifest in ignorant comments, stereotyped perspectives, and hateful language. Cliven Bundy, the cattle rancher from Nevada, is a racist—listen to his ravings! And since you (and I) aren't bigots like that, we can glibly claim a higher moral ground: "I'm not a racist!" But here's the fatal problem with that: "racism" also means the structures of white supremacy and the institutional practices of oppression based on race. And so the question isn't whether you're a bigot who spews out backward and dull-witted language, but what you're doing to keep an eye on policy or law, and how you're working to dismantle the institutional and structural expressions of white supremacy in your classroom or in the broader community.

The well-spring of bigotry and racial prejudice is the structure of inequality itself, not the other way around. That is, the reality of inequality baked into law and economic condition as well as history, custom, and culture generates racist thoughts and feelings as justification, and those racist ideas keep regenerating as long as the structures of white supremacy and Black oppression are in place. Race itself is, of course, both everywhere and nowhere at all—a social construction and massive fiction, and at the same time, the hardest of hard-edged realities.

Donald Sterling uttered the N-word and lost his NBA franchise, but his wealth came from decades as a slumlord, and that didn't warrant any sanction whatsoever from the powerful. The mayor of

Chicago shuttered more than fifty public schools in predominantly Black and poor communities while he militarized a bloated and aggressive police force, covered up police murders in Black communities, and never used the N-word. This is white supremacy and racist practice on the ground and in the world. Call it its name.

I often provoked my students, saying, "Do you know that a mile from our school there are fifteen thousand Irishmen [or Jewish women] living in cages?" "Come on! No way!" There was always a general sense of disbelief, and a notion that maybe I was joking. "You're kidding, right?"

Well, I wasn't being fully honest, so let me change that—"Do you know that one mile from our campus there are fifteen thousand young Black and Latinx men living in cages?" "No, I didn't know that, but I'm not completely surprised either; what crimes did they commit?" The fact of Black and Brown men being imprisoned is part of the known world, the common sense of recognized things, normalized to the point of invisibility—you didn't know that, you say; indeed, you didn't even *notice* that. So in another sense, you *did* know it.

A truth-telling young history teacher I know in Chicago engaged his class in a required lesson on the famous *Brown v. Board of Education* Supreme Court decision ending racial segregation in public schools, and it quickly became anything but standard and expected. The class was all students of color, mostly African American and a few Latinx. The scripted lesson was designed to illustrate our great upward path as a progressive nation, but when one student piped up and said, "So, you're saying this class is against the law, right? Can I call the cops?" everyone cracked up at the obvious contradiction of attending a racially segregated school while learning that segregation was outlawed sixty years earlier. Over the next few weeks the students and their teacher went dramatically off-road, studying white flight and red-lining, various strategies and tactics white communities (including communities in Chicago) employed to resist racial integration, reading Ta-Nehisi Coates and Nikole Hannah-Jones, and documenting the failure of the mayor and his appointed school board to take meaningful steps to overcome the injustice. They presented their findings to the school community and eventually to the Board of Education, and this sparked the development of a city-wide student group, Students Against Racism (STAR).

We must face reality and courageously confront history, tell the truth, and then destroy the entire edifice of white supremacy: metaphorically speaking, it means burning down the plantation.

And when the plantation is at last burned to the ground, people of European descent, or "those Americans who believe that they are white," will find the easy privileges we've taken for granted disappearing, and along with them our willful blindness and faux innocence.[1] Also gone will be the fragile, precarious perch of superiority. What a relief! White folks will give up our accumulated, unearned advantages and yet stand to gain something better: a fuller personhood and a moral bearing. We face an urgent challenge, then, if we are to join humanity in the enormous task of creating a just and caring world, and it begins with rejecting white supremacy—not simply despising bigotry and backwardness, but spurning as well all those despicable structures and traditions. It extends to refusing to embrace optics over justice, "multiculturalism" or "diversity" over an honest reckoning with reality—to becoming race traitors as we learn the loving art of solidarity in practice.

There's a somewhat similar challenge facing men, and it, too, requires facing up to reality, examining history courageously and thoroughly, and noting the interaction of prejudice and sexism with the structures that uphold and spread the bias: the system of male supremacy. It, too, will demand that we burn down a plantation of sorts, and it, too, will mean the privileged—all men—will lose their comfortable and taken-for-granted advantages, as well as their shaky and inherently unstable place of dominance.

The Arts of Liberty and Transformative Possibilities

I want to expand the power of my students—agency is a universal human endowment and an essential power, and self-education is consequential precisely because it requires and represents the exercise of agency. I tell my students that as part of the great flow of human history, as inheritors and creators of culture, they can each learn everything—and any classroom that discourages or disallows the full expression of students' agency is restricting humanity. I want to move a step beyond noting that they can look at the world through critical lenses; I want them to know that they need no one's permission to interrogate the world, no one else's reading list to comprehend the world, and no one's approval to link arms with others in order to change things. Students should leave every class with their imaginations nourished and their curiosities engaged—they should have experienced the ecstasy of creation, the joy of making something from the materials at hand.

Emily Dickinson wrote that "imagination ignites the slow fuse of possibility." Gwendolyn Brooks asked, "Does man love art?" Her answer, "Man visits art but cringes. Art hurts. Art urges voyages."

The voyages art demands lie at the very heart of our humanness: journeys in search of new solutions to old problems, explorations of spirit spaces and emotional landscapes, trips into the hidden meanings and elaborate schemes we construct to make our lives understandable and endurable, flights hooked on metaphor and analogy, wobbly rambles away from the cold reality of the world we inhabit—the world as such—into worlds that could be or should be standing just beyond the horizon. These are the voyages that foreground the capacities and features that mark us as uniquely human: aspiration, self-awareness, projection, desire, ingenuity, courage and compassion and commitment—all of these and more are harvests of our imaginations.

But it's also true—art hurts. The capacity to see the world as if it could be otherwise creates yearning and liberates desire—we are freed (or condemned) to run riot. Imagination—necessarily subversive, unruly, and disruptive—challenges the *status quo* simply by opening us up to consider alternatives; suddenly the taken-for-granted and the given world become choices and no longer warrant life (or death?) sentences.

When the aim of education is the reproduction of all the social relations as they are now, schooling is nothing more than locating oneself on the grand pyramid of winners and losers. When school is geared to the absorption of facts, learning becomes exclusively and exhaustively selfish, and there is no obvious social motive for it. The measure of success is competitive—people are turned against one another, and every difference becomes a score for somebody and a deficit for someone else. Getting ahead of others is the primary goal in such places, and mutual assistance, which can be so entirely natural in other human affairs, is severely restricted or banned.

But where a curriculum of questioning, studying, researching, and undertaking active work in the community is the order of the day, helping others is not a form of charity, an act that, intentionally or not, impoverishes both recipient and benefactor. Rather, a spirit of open communication, interchange, and analysis is an expression of love and becomes more commonplace. In these places there is a certain natural disorder, some anarchy and chaos, as there is in any busy workshop. But there is also a sense of joy, and a deeper discipline at work, the discipline of getting things done and learning through life with one another. We see clearly in these cases that education at its best is always generative—in a way that training, for example, never can be—and that offering knowledge and learning and education to others diminishes nothing for oneself.

The comprehensive demand on students and teachers alike is this: You must change. You are living in the world as it is, of course, but right next to the world-as-such lie worlds that could be or should be but are not yet. We are products of this world, but as we reach toward a possible world, or as we work to create a more joyful and just, peaceful and loving world right here, we must simultaneously change ourselves.

Change yourself, change the world; change yourself in order to change the world; change yourself to be worthy of the advancing world.

Where are we on the clock of the universe? What does it mean to be human in the twenty-first century? Who am I in relation to others? What kind of a society do we want to create? Where do we go from here? Our classrooms can be generative sites of contention, of push and pull and authentic engagement as we take on first questions and fundamental principles. And when these questions animate teachers and students in their projects and pursuits, freedom comes into view as something attainable and real.

On one wall I post another poem by Ms. Brooks, this one a fragment from an homage to Paul Robeson:

> *. . . we are each other's*
> *harvest:*
> *we are each other's*
> *business:*
> *we are each other's*
> *magnitude and bond.*

If we hope to move beyond our precarious pockets of good work—if we're to connect with other teachers and broader communities of concern in order to accompany the coming generations and assist in creating a mighty movement for enlightenment and liberation, love and justice in our schools and in the larger society—we must identify those far-flung fragments, and name the commitments that unite us and the principles around which we can organize and mobilize.

How do we see ourselves and our problems/challenges/potentials? How can we connect our personal pursuits with a collective search for a better world for all? How can we live with one foot in the mud and muck of the world as it is while the other foot stretches toward a world that could be but is not yet? How can we transform ourselves to be worthy of the profound social transformations we desire and need? And how can we build within ourselves the thoughtfulness, compassion, and courage to dive into the wreckage all around us on a mission of repair?

There is only one way to begin: We open our eyes. We pay attention. We're astonished at the beauty in every direction as well as the unnecessary suffering on all sides. We release our imaginations. We act. We doubt and rethink, and we start again.

Repeat for a lifetime.

Notes

1. Ta-Nehisi Coates, *Between the World and Me* (New York: Spiegel & Grau, 2015), 6.

Teaching Politics in the Age of Trump

Justin Christensen

Justin Christensen has taught Advanced Placement government classes for ten years at St. Ignatius College Preparatory in San Francisco, California. In 2013, he co-founded a Twitter community of government teachers at #hsgovchat.

LIKE MANY TEACHERS ALL OVER THE COUNTRY, I STOP AT A LOCAL CAFE every morning for my cherished daily cup of coffee.

As I waited for my coffee one morning in March, I scrolled through my Twitter feed and discovered that Donald Trump had yet again fired off tweets the previous night that were getting a lot of attention. The first was a veiled threat to "spill the beans" on another candidate's wife, and the other seemed to promote fear of an entire religion.

I would be in front of my students in ninety minutes. Should I show these tweets in class today? What should I say if a student asked me about them?

Before I got in my car, I took screenshots of both tweets and posed a question to my colleagues on Twitter: "As teachers, how do we respond when (Trump)'s statements would break our own classroom rules?"

Lyin' Ted Cruz just used a picture of Melania from a G.Q. shoot in his ad. Be careful, Lyin' Ted, or I will spill the beans on your wife!
—@realDonaldTrump, 3/22/16, 6:53 p.m.

Incompetent Hillary, despite the horrible attack in Brussels
today, wants borders to be weak and open—and let the Muslims
flow in. No way!
—@realDonaldTrump, 3/22/16, 7:59 p.m.

I did not often encounter this dilemma when I taught AP government during the previous two presidential elections. I happily
presented both sides to my students. In 2012, I even bought cutouts
of Barack Obama and Mitt Romney. I would stand next to each cutout and act as their spokesman. Since my students tended to support
Barack Obama, I spent more time speaking on behalf of Romney.
I wanted my students to listen to both sides in order to develop an
informed opinion.

This year, I have yet to buy a cutout of Donald Trump. As I tried
to explain in my tweet that morning, I was uncomfortable acting as
a spokesman for someone who would routinely break my own standards if he were a student in my class.

For example, he would fail to meet my expectation that students
treat each other with respect and avoid profane language. Trump has
mocked a reporter with a disability. He has criticized the appearance of
Carly Fiorina, Megyn Kelly, and Heidi Cruz. He has said he will "beat
the s— out of" ISIS. He has stated that he would "like to punch (a pro-
tester) in the face." He has even alluded to his own personal anatomy.

I also expect my students to use facts to defend their claims. The
editor of PolitiFact, which fact-checks claims by politicians, found
that Trump's "record on truth and accuracy is astonishingly poor."[1]

When I posted my tweet that morning, my colleagues on Twitter
began to weigh in. Here are a few examples:

Use them as exs. of immature, abusive rhetoric, unfit for civil
discourse on any level. That's not taking sides.
—@DocStar11, 3/23/16, 1:11 a.m.

I transition to the Separation of Powers as a safety net when I
feel like bias is coming out.
—@engdkyl, 3/23/16, 8:27 p.m.

thanks for talking about this I talk about free speech u may not agree with what he has to say but he has the right to say it
—@PollackWTW, 3/29/16, 1:21 p.m.

Thanks to the Twitter community of teachers that use #hsgovchat and #sschat, I discovered that I was not alone. Other teachers are also wondering how to facilitate conversations about Trump in their classrooms.

So how should we teach government in the age of Trump? Since that early March morning at the cafe, I have developed five helpful questions to ask my students.

1. *When does Trump's rhetoric contradict our classroom rules?* We need to explicitly name such examples, otherwise our students may misinterpret our silence as support for such language in our schools.
2. *Why does Trump use controversial rhetoric?* Invite students to analyze the media industry and research how much free media he received.
3. *What does polling reveal about the coalition of supporters Trump has created?* We must invite our students to understand his appeal and analyze its deeper causes.
4. *What do experts think of Trump's proposals (such as deporting eleven million undocumented immigrants or bringing back waterboarding)?* We should ask our students to fact-check and evaluate his claims.
5. *How does Trump fit in the Republican Party?* We should remind our students that Trump does not speak for many conservatives or Republicans. For example, students should hear Speaker Paul Ryan's response to Trump's proposal to ban Muslims from entering the country: "This is not conservatism. What was proposed is not what this party stands for."[2]

Taken together, these five questions have helped me navigate discussions about Trump in my classroom. In our schools, we create expectations for how we talk to each another, conduct research, and develop an informed opinion. We must enforce these classroom expectations, even if a presidential candidate breaks them.

Notes

1. Angie Drobnic Holan, "All Politicians Lie. Some More Than Others," *New York Times*, December 11, 2015.

2. Jay Newton-Small, "Speaker Paul Ryan Condemns Donald Trump's Ban on Muslims," *Time*, December 8, 2015.

The Three Illusions: Teaching Children to Be Change Makers

Julia Putnam

Julia Putnam is the principal and co-founder of the James and Grace Lee Boggs School in Detroit, Michigan. A former classroom teacher and writer-in-residence for the InsideOut Literary Arts program, she uses her expertise in youth development and community organizing to work with teachers, parents, and students on creating and maintaining positive school culture and ambitious instruction.

I BELIEVE THAT WHEN STUDENTS LEARN ABOUT THE ROOT CAUSES OF the things they see around them, they begin to understand how they can impact things for the better. They become change makers. There is no one more determined to work toward justice than a kid who thinks something is unfair.

I think often about how real change might happen at the Boggs School. In his piece "Democracy Is Not a Supermarket," author and journalist Anand Giridharadas writes that real change escapes many change makers in part because of three illusions that misguide the way they attempt to enact change.[1]

The first illusion he calls the Starfish Illusion. You know the story about the guy who throws beached starfish back in the ocean one at a time? His friend says, "What difference does it make?" and the guy says, while throwing in a starfish, "Well, it makes a difference to that one." Anand says that this creates the illusion that we can save one starfish, or one person, at a time without examining the ways in which we are complicit in the problem they need saving from. At the Boggs School, we are conscious of attempting to educate kids while finding ways to save us all from what this country calls education. We do an incredible job of making sure that kids feel loved and heard and respected, of helping them even to feel entitled to respect while also asking them to return that respect to others. And all the while that they're feeling loved and respected and protected, we also say, "Take this state test that is going to ask you about the specific tools used by the Potawatomi man, but nothing about colonization and how the colonists treated the indigenous communities who lived here and shaped our land."

We ask the kids to face the dissonance of knowing a lot about their communities and being told by test results that they know little. We tell them that the test does not measure their intelligence, but then again it could mean the difference between having a school or not. A loving and engaging school may save some kids, but we all remain complicit in a society that necessitates our kids needing to be saved in the first place.

There are many ways that, by being a school that follows the rules, we still are very much of the system and we must stay aware of that.

The second illusion Anand points out is the illusion that you can change the world without changing people. We believe we can congratulate ourselves on being "woke" and deride and discard those without the equivalent political and social understanding that we have. But, Anand wonders, is there space for those he calls the "still-waking"?

We have high expectations for our kids—so much so that we are often surprised, upset, and defeated when they make mistakes, especially if those mistakes are egregious and heavy. Earlier this year, one of our Spanish teachers, Ms. Jazmin—who is from an organization that equips schools with language teachers and teaches at Boggs once a week—left our sixth-grade classroom in tears. The kids were without their usual aide and they took this moment to unleash their worst on this vulnerable teacher. They responded to her Spanish prompts in gibberish. They laughed at and made fun of her accent. Some told her to go back to her country. And they began throwing paper around the room. When Ms. Jazmin realized she wouldn't be able to get the kids' attention back and that their behavior was escalating, she went to get our school secretary, apologetic for needing help. When an adult that the kids knew came into the room, there was absolute, shame-filled silence.

When I heard about the incident, I was ashamed, too. How could I be in charge of a school in which this could happen? What are we doing wrong? Another of the co-founders of the school, Marisol, and I agonized over what to do. We were both comforted by something my husband, Peter, said: "Jules, the Boggs School isn't special because nothing bad happens, it's special because of how you all respond when bad things happen."

Marisol and I decided on a plan to respond. We've been learning how to implement restorative justice practices at the school and had been practicing peace circles throughout the year. Marisol had the first peace circle with the kids and invited their families. A series of questions were asked, one at a time, in the circle: What were you thinking and feeling when it was happening? What are you thinking and feeling right now? How can we make this right?

Many of the children expressed not being sure what to do in the moment, even though they knew what was happening was not right. They didn't want to be seen as tattletales and things happened so quickly, they said. Some of the children said they thought it would be funny at the time, but they quickly understood their behavior was inappropriate, began to feel bad, but didn't know how to pull it back. The parents who attended expressed disappointment and anger. One mom realized that she'd taught her child to be proud of his own culture, but hadn't exposed him to enough other cultures so that he'd know that his was not the only one that needed to be respected.

One mom had grown up speaking Spanish. She said that she had friends as a child, but that when others made fun of her accent, her friends said nothing. She went on, "When I asked my daughter what she did to stand up for that teacher and she said 'Nothing,' it broke my heart." Everyone, adult and child, got to speak their piece and be heard.

In their next class, Marisol helped the kids craft apology letters that would truly speak to the remorse they felt and that was expressed in the first circle. The letters were given to Ms. Jazmin after the second peace circle was planned, this one with Ms. Jazmin in attendance. The same questions were asked. When it was Ms. Jazmin's turn to say what she was thinking and feeling, she said that she was thinking that her accent was too thick and that she should work on improving her English pronunciations. She said that she wondered if teaching was the right profession for her and what she'd done wrong.

The kids were horrified that she took responsibility for their behavior. During their turns to speak, they begged her not to work on her accent because it was "what made her interesting." They vowed to be their best selves in her classroom and to embrace learning Spanish as a way to open their minds. Ms. Jazmin said that she'd never been part of a conversation like this at a school before and she was so grateful. She told them that they were really good kids and she was excited to come back for the next lesson.

Restorative practices allow us to believe that anyone has the capacity to change; they respect the capacity for human beings to grow, and we owe it to children and maybe to ourselves and other adults to give everyone that chance. There are definite mindsets that must evolve for our world to change for the better, but that doesn't happen overnight and it doesn't happen without practice. What if that practice were happening in our schools?

The third illusion is that you can change the world without being rooted in it. In the documentary film *American Revolutionary: The Evolution of Grace Lee Boggs*, a young college student asks the legendary Detroit-based activist Grace Lee Boggs how she stays motivated and positive when we are all working on such despairing cases of injustice. Grace responded: "I stayed involved because I stayed in one place for the last fifty-five years. I grew to love Detroit and to feel responsible for Detroit so that I was able to grow. And trying one thing after another and trying to learn from everything I tried . . . the illusion that there's a quick answer leads to burnout."

I am so often frustrated by how far we have yet to go at the Boggs School. I am grateful when I am reminded we aren't getting it all wrong. The silliness and laughter of the kids reminds me to remember to be joyful and to lighten up and have fun. Grace once said she was grateful to have lived one hundred years because you see time differently and you understand how much reality is changing all the time, even if you cannot see it happening.

And so I desperately want a school that offers a robust and flexible, yet predictable, curriculum with healthy delicious food cooked on-site by students with adult staff to support them, and a school social worker and counselor and restorative justice coordinator who ensure that along with the rich and stimulating academic curriculum, there will also be a robust and effective social-emotional curriculum, and a roomy campus with a working farm tended to by students, staff, and families together, where no person would feel marginalized from the community; a place where each child would graduate with the ability to provide tours to people both in the school and around the community because they know the place so deeply that it will always be home no matter where they go; where students would be at the forefront of curriculum development, community peace-keeping, local policy initiatives, and joyous and educational community event-planning; where the neighbors around the school would know the community more deeply because of the knowledge and skill-sharing the students would engage in, and the kids will know the neighbors because they'd be invited into the school to share their skills and stories, but I know that this will take time and effort and change.

Bob Moses—one of the leaders of the Student Nonviolent Coordinating Committee (SNCC)—once said that it wasn't hard to register a sharecropper in 1960 Mississippi to vote. The difficulty was that so many systems needed to change in order for a sharecropper in 1960 Mississippi to vote. For the vision I mention above (which is only the beginning of what could be), so many systems would need to change. And that systems change will take time, probably more than the five years that the Boggs School has been open so far. It may take fifty-five years, which is beyond what I will probably get to see.

The things that make it hard to change the current educational system are definitely the ways in which this current, inhumane system clings and fights to continue to exist, even within us. This is why, when we asked Grace's permission to name the school after her and Jimmy, she challenged us to think beyond what we even believe is possible.

I don't know what kind of change—real change—the Boggs School is making or will ultimately make. I do know that when I was just sixteen years old, there were some adults who cared enough about my opinion to ask me what I thought about the world and the way it was. I'd already been thinking about those things but no one—certainly no one in school—had ever thought to ask. That interest in me as a teenager evolved into my part in the founding of the Boggs School. What might our interest in our kids today evolve into? I am excited to stick around and find out for as many years as I am able.

Notes

1. Anand Giridharadas, "Democracy Is Not a Supermarket," Medium, October 31, 2017.

Standing Up Against Hate

Mica Pollock

*Mica Pollock is the director of the Center for Research on Educational
Equity, Assessment, and Teaching Excellence (CREATE) at the
University of California, San Diego, the author of three books
including* Schooltalk: Rethinking What We Say About—and to—
Students Every Day, *and the editor of* Everyday Antiracism.

EDUCATORS HAVE MANY RESPONSIBILITIES. THE URGENCY OF THREE OF
these has been heightened recently:

- Stand up against hate and intimidation, so schools stay safe
  for learning;
- engage the facts; and
- protect the right to learn.

We've always had those responsibilities; they're just more necessary
now than ever.

These past years have been fraught for students, teachers, and
schools. We've seen a spike in incidents of hate and bias on K–12
and college campuses nationwide. It's becoming obvious that every
insult overheard on the nightly news, every tweet forwarded on social media, and every slur scrawled on a building can have mounting
consequences for students and schools. Public figures are explicitly
threatening many students' rights and communities. Students are

repeating these threats and claims to one another, sometimes without fully understanding them.

And simultaneously, some educators are getting labeled "partisan" when they simply challenge hate or bullying on their own campuses—or engage students in dialogue about real, controversial issues, or just affirm that all students have the right to learn safely in school.

This reality places a burden on educators, to be sure. But no matter what our politics are, standing up against hate—and for learning—is the basic work of education. And who better than teachers to facilitate this?

Stand Up Against Hate and Intimidation

We're in an era of escalating hate and threats toward many of the young people and communities we serve. Undocumented and refugee students have been told that the president wants them out. The federal government is sending the message that schools don't have to honor LGBT students' identities. Boys have heard that disrespecting girls is okay. We've all heard racist, Islamophobic, and xenophobic talk become more commonplace, accompanied by targeted policies. These sentiments get repeated on our campuses. Hate-filled violence is on the rise.

And as educators, it's our job to denounce hate and intimidation where we work, to make sure students feel safe to learn.

The U.S. Constitution protects a range of free-expression rights in schools. Freedom of speech protects us all, so we don't simply outlaw all "offensive" ideas from our schools. But we don't allow true threats of harm in schools, either, because schools must remain safe for learning. Our civil rights laws also require educators to protect public school students from harassment based on race, color, national origin, sex, religion, or disability; a school has a responsibility to maintain a safe and nondiscriminatory learning environment for all students. When hostile environments impede student learning, educators must take action to end the harassment, eliminate any hostile environment and its effects, and prevent the harassment from recurring.

Put these points together, and we see that schools are places where hateful speech and action, harassment and violence are supposed to be challenged, not ignored. As educators, we are both legally and morally responsible for fostering learning environments where people aren't denigrated and threatened so that students can participate in and benefit from school.

Educators must always model what it looks like to be an "upstander": to stand up in the moment to challenge hateful speech and call instead for learning and respect. And the primary antidote to hate is preventive speech: continually talking about how to respect and value other human beings every day.

The triage work of educators is to challenge hate—to ask speakers to respect and value others so all can learn. The longer-term work is to prevent hateful activity on campus. And the longest-term, most powerful work is to make our resistance to hate routine, by consistently asking whether the most ordinary words we use in schools and society distort, misunderstand, misrepresent, denigrate, or devalue people.

Here Are a Few Ideas for How to Prevent Hateful Activity on Campus

- State, publicly and often, that harassment and intimidation have no place in our schools and that our campuses respect and value everyone so everyone can learn.
- Share powerful statements about the value of diversity and inclusivity written by K–12 or university administrators, educators, or students.
- Display posters articulating that, while hate is not welcome at our schools, students and ideas are.
- Partner with local organizations to spread anti-hate messaging.
- Refuse to downplay slurs and hateful speech as inconsequential events.
- Showcase inspiring examples of schools, communities, teachers, and students resisting hate, promoting dialogue, and building relationships.

- Bring effective tools for open dialogue to our schools such as restorative justice circles, Socratic dialogues, and basic scaffolds for classroom dialogue about controversial topics. Explicitly teach the skill of discussing opposing views.
- Engage the facts.

The foundational work of counteracting hate is addressing the everyday forms of bias and misinformation all around us—for example, the deeper, routine misconceptions about the "types of people" referred to by the N-word, or who the swastika is meant to exclude, and who that anti-immigrant scrawl on the ground purports to describe. Pursuing accurate claims and a more informed understanding of our students, communities, country, and world is actually key to educational equity effort of all kinds. Hate, bias, and passivity toward harm to others all thrive on a lack of knowledge. We stand up for one another when we get more informed about fellow human beings and the world.

To counter the stereotypes and misinformation that seep into all of us, educators need to facilitate learning: about historical realities; about the shape of contemporary wealth, poverty, and employment; about who landed here and why; and about the opportunities folks actually get or don't get in the United States. With our students, colleagues, and even with ourselves, we need to question old myths that value some "types of people" over others; we need to learn the history of our nation and the facts about the people we hear some of our politicians denigrate.

To create this fact base, and to build the relationships that unite us, we also need to seek deeper knowledge about real, complex lives. That means knowing the realities that motivated neighbors to take the risk of immigrating or seeking refuge; the diversity that exists within religions or "races"; and the personal facts about people's real lives, struggles, hard work, contributions, talents, and hopes.

No matter what our politics are, standing up against hate—and for learning—is the basic work of education.

These shifts all begin with questioning what we typically say and what we think we know. Harvard professor Ali Asani poses a wonderful starter question to students in our times: "How do you know what you know about Islam?"

Educators can make a difference by engaging in a daily quest to counteract misinformation with learning. In an era when the value of facts seems up for debate, educators need to trade in solid data and true human stories.

Notably, as educators engage the facts, we'll find ourselves holding our students and ourselves to a higher standard than the many public figures who are ready to disregard facts altogether. But now more than ever, we can't back down from the quest to learn.

Engaging evidence is, of course, central to the Common Core State Standards and Next Generation Science Standards, which ask us to help students make evidence-based arguments in all grades and subjects. And crucially, striving for accuracy in describing other people, social issues, and our country is not being "politically correct." Engaging in the quest for evidence and inquiry is education itself— and necessary for democracy to function. In a nation where many adults are too polarized in their thinking to learn, schools may be the last place where Americans are asked to talk about and engage new information.

Protect the Right to Learn

As we embark on the long-haul work of counteracting hate and engaging facts, educators are also faced increasingly with the task of protecting students' basic right to learn—and our own ability to teach about solid information, complicated social issues, and real lives.

The number of stories about teachers asked to discontinue instructional activities is growing by the day. (Consider the teacher in New York who was told not to engage in a long-standing, historically grounded lesson about Columbus Day because it was "too controversial," or the Oregon teacher who got a letter from parents angry that she might say something negative about Trump when teaching about the Magna Carta.) More than ever, administrators today need to support teachers' own ability to engage the facts and analyze issues across perspectives, while teachers need to build skills in supporting students to explore tough ideas.

Today, along with preventing harassment in school, the work of protecting the right to learn also increasingly includes insisting on 1) the value of public education itself; 2) the right of every child to attend a publicly funded school accountable for supporting all students; and 3) the protection of students' other basic civil rights in schools (e.g., the rights of undocumented immigrants and students with disabilities; student rights under Title VI and Title IX; and more).

Protecting the right to learn is the basic work of education. And to develop the next generation, we can't avoid facts and issues in classrooms because they are fraught, or rope off inquiry into real-world issues as too political to discuss. Doing so would, as a student in San Diego, California, put it, leave young people "unprepared for participating in democracy."

Educators in public schools are not supposed to be politically partisan. But that word requires clarification today. Educators in Arlington, Virginia, have been critiqued for hanging up signs with phrases like "Diversity strengthens us" and "Science is real." The parents who complained called those messages too partisan and political for school. And so, we arrive at our deepest core tension.[1]

Because some government actors have promoted intolerance and distorted facts, teachers who speak up against hate or for students, facts, and learning are accused of being "politically partisan."

Educators must stand together to resist this message. Standing up to hate is not partisan. Studying facts is not partisan. Learning about the experiences of real people is not partisan. All of these actions form the core of a U.S. education.

As we resist hate and everyday bias—and engage fraught national issues and facts gracefully and earnestly in our classrooms—educators will glue the nation back together in the months and years to come. While others in the United States have stopped engaging across perspectives, educators and students are some of the last people still trying! And everything we say has the power to shape the future of our children and our nation.

We're better equipped for the job than anybody else: engaging in dialogue across perspectives is our job. And we can further equip ourselves and one another for the task by sharing the many resources produced by support organizations and the ways we are working on everything above in our classroom, school buildings, and communities. It just takes effort, resource sharing, and a commitment to growth.

It's an incredible time to be an educator. Let's support each other in this work.

Notes

1. Heather Hunter, "Virginia School Board Defends Politically Correct Signs in Classrooms," *Daily Caller*, February 8, 2017.

Yes, Race and Politics Belong in the Classroom: Ten Tips for Teachers on How to Engage Students in Difficult Conversations

H. Richard Milner IV

*H. Richard Milner IV is the director of the Center for Urban
Education at the University of Pittsburgh and editor-in-chief of
the journal* Urban Education. *He is the author of* Start Where
You Are, But Don't Stay There *and* Rac(e)ing to Class.

THE 2016 PRESIDENTIAL-ELECTION SEASON AND THE SUBSEQUENT PRESI-
dency of Donald Trump have recentered serious issues of gender,
race, immigration, and social class for people in the United States and
beyond its borders. But the issues themselves are not the only areas of
concern. The digressive manner in which people are engaging each
other is concerning as well.

Recently, Elise, my seven-year-old daughter, walked into the room
as I watched a heated conversation about immigration on a popular
national news channel and asked me: "Why are people so mad at each
other?" I reassured her that people were not necessarily mad at each
other as much as they were passionate about their views on the topic.
With a look of confusion and a bit of disbelief, Elise walked out of the

room. I knew I had missed an important opportunity—a teachable moment.

Middle and high school teachers continue sharing with me that their students are also grappling with confusion and disbelief during moments of stark opposition on political, social, racial, and economic issues. And while these teachers recognize the potential value of discussing these areas of dissonance with their students, they struggle less about what they should address than how to engage their students in ways that are powerfully constructive. They often feel that they are missing important opportunities for students to think, engage with each other, learn, and develop; although children of all ages are reflecting on tough social issues, many opportunities for teachers to draw upon these powerful realities as anchors for curriculum and instruction are lost.

Rather than avoiding controversial matters, teachers (and parents) should instead deliberately keep them at the center of classroom instruction. But if teachers aren't properly prepared to engage their students productively, we can actually do more harm than good. With appropriate tools, we as educators have an opportunity to not only build lessons that connect to students' interests, but perhaps shepherd them into becoming deeply engaged citizens who work against racism, sexism, and other forms of discrimination.

But many educators who recognize the potential power of this engagement do not know how to foster it. How do we support teachers so they can create a classroom environment that cultivates, instead of stifles, difficult discussions about race, class, politics, and culture? Often, the very issues we ignore are the ones on which we should focus the most.

Here are ten recommendations for my fellow teachers as they develop a classroom ethos that encourages, advances, and addresses the toughest issues students face inside and outside of the classroom:

1. From the very beginning of the academic year, design a classroom ethos that is open to questioning, open to varying perspectives, and that encourages discourse. Creating an environment of respect (even when conversations get

heated) is essential to encouraging students to interrogate and grapple with tough issues.

2. Reflect on your personal views and positions on race and society. Your goal is not to indoctrinate students into believing or embracing a particular point of view. The goal is not for teachers to push their own agendas, but rather to explore nuances with students to sharpen their analytic and critical-thinking skills, which are transferable to other situations. Offer counterviews to students' positions as they participate in classroom discussion; expect and encourage students to do the same. By sharing alternative views, relying on publications from across the political spectrum, and inviting guest speakers to share their positions on issues, you can support students as they strengthen their own arguments, perhaps shift their perspective, and hopefully understand another point of view.

3. Draw from current affairs as a jumping-off point for tough talk. The Charlottesville terror attack committed by white supremacists, recent high-profile police-involved shootings across the country, Colin Kaepernick's refusal to stand during the national anthem and the subsequent backlash from the NFL, regulatory changes to affirmative action programs recently reported to be under consideration by the U.S. Department of Justice, ongoing national immigration debates, and the Flint, Michigan, water crisis are all current examples of how race might be explored inside the classroom.

4. Identify and centralize the facts, based on evidence from varying sources and multiple points of view. Encourage and require students to explore different sources of information and to consider positions and standpoints inconsistent with their initial thinking on topics.

5. Expect students to draw from a variety of sources, including their own personal experiences and diverse news coverage, to aid them in expressing and substantiating their viewpoints and positions.

6. Design instructions for conversations to logically connect to the in-school curriculum. As teachers, you should prepare students to understand convergences between societal matters and the content being taught in school.

7. Build your own repertoire of skills to support tough talk in the classroom. Be prepared to respond to the cognitive, social-emotional, and affective needs of students as conversations emerge. Build networks to support student needs that fall outside your toolkit by working with school counselors, psychologists, social workers, and others.

8. Recognize and nurture the social-emotional impact of these conversations on students, who could feel very strongly about a topic or issue and become emotional as conversations develop. Acknowledge and validate these students' feelings and respond to them with affirmation and sensitivity. While acknowledging their feelings, however, do not let students off the hook if they express or advocate hate, phobias, or various other "isms."

9. Talk, collaborate, and partner with parents, community members, and school administrators to understand their views and expectations regarding difficult classroom discussions. Develop strategies with those groups—especially families and communities—to bolster and complement discourse inside and outside the classroom.

10. Work toward healing and consider next steps associated with tough talk. Once students have engaged with the issues and deepened their knowledge, help them think about their role in working to build a more just society, provide space for students to heal, and rebuild their psychological well-being. In other words, what can students (and any of us) do to fight discrimination and create an equitable society for all?

As teachers, we are under an enormous amount of pressure to teach a curriculum that is tied to accountability systems, such as standardized testing. Thus, it may seem difficult to talk about contemporary issues inside the classroom when such learning and engagement can be seen as inconsequential to what students may think we're supposed to be teaching. But for many students, the tough social topics are the curriculum of their lives and thus should be addressed inside the classroom. Until we address the toughest of these realities—particularly race and racism—in our schools and society, we cannot hope to achieve a democracy that truly is for all.

Safety
Matters

Cops or Counselors?
Responding to the Threat of School
Shootings with Care Rather Than Fear

Pedro A. Noguera

Pedro A. Noguera is a professor of education and the director for the Center for the Transformation of Schools at UCLA. He is a sociologist, the author of twelve books, and appears regularly as an education commentator on CNN, MSNBC, National Public Radio, and other national news outlets.

JUST OVER ONE MONTH AFTER THE MASS SHOOTINGS AT STONEMAN Douglas High School in Parkland, Florida, on February 14, 2018, another shooting incident occurred at Great Mills High School in southern Maryland. In both incidents, multiple individuals were killed or injured, the schools were placed under lockdown, and local law enforcement was called to respond to the violence. Although far more people were killed or injured at Stoneman Douglas than at Great Mills, the fact that the two incidents occurred during such a short time period reinforced fears that the nation was in the midst of an epidemic of school-based violence.

In the first three months of 2018 there were seventeen school shootings (at schools ranging from kindergarten through college level) in which one person was either killed or injured. According to Everytown, a national gun-control advocacy group, there have been over three hundred school shootings since the massacre at Sandy

Hook in December 2012, at which twenty children (first graders) and six adults were killed. There have also been dozens of threats that have resulted in schools being closed or placed under lockdown. Almost all of these were false alarms, but in this heightened period of awareness and anxiety, every threat is taken seriously.

The mass shooting in Parkland, Florida, has sparked a flood of legislative and executive responses aimed at deterring future assaults. Some of these may seem eerily familiar: improved background checks on all individuals who seek to purchase a weapon, a ban on bump stocks (a device used to convert a semiautomatic weapon into one capable of rapid fire), limiting access to assault weapons, etc. They are familiar because after each mass shooting—in Las Vegas and Aurora, Colorado, etc.—they are proposed and debated again. Of course, all of these proposals have been opposed by the powerful National Rifle Association, which has taken the position that almost any effort to limit access to guns is an attack on the Second Amendment. Because of this organization's intensive lobbying and the pressure it applies on lawmakers, there has been relatively little change in our nation's gun laws despite the carnage.

Perhaps the mass shooting at Stoneman Douglas, and the marches by young people across the nation that followed, will change that. In an effort to circumvent new gun control laws, President Trump called for teachers and other school personnel to be armed. Though hardly a well-thought-out proposal, the president's call immediately captured the media's attention and sparked a raging debate over how best to prevent the next shooting. Within weeks, several jurisdictions heeded the president's call and policies allowing school personnel to carry weapons were adopted. This occurred even as there were several reports of school personnel misusing weapons on school grounds, and in some cases, accidentally injuring children. Yet, in an atmosphere where fear seems to be growing, many people feel that doing something, even if it is controversial, poorly conceived, and largely symbolic, seems better than doing nothing at all.

What Is to Be Done? Understanding the Nature of the Problem

The threat of school shootings has understandably sparked a search for effective solutions that would ensure the safety of children and teachers in schools. The "unalienable rights" to life, liberty, and the pursuit of happiness, guaranteed in the Declaration of Independence, are, after all, even more fundamental and basic than the Second Amendment "right to bear arms." The need to create assurances that the safety of children when they are at school can be guaranteed is particularly important given their vulnerability and the fact that they are mandated by law to attend school.

Yet, despite the unquestionable need for school safety, finding ways to bring it about has proven to be complicated and confounding. Part of the problem lies in a lack of objective knowledge about the nature of school shootings themselves.

Despite the similarities between the incidents at Stoneman Douglas and Great Mills High Schools (i.e., multiple people killed by a shooter at school), closer examination reveals that they were actually quite different. While mass shootings—which have been defined by a Congressional Research Service report on the subject as a "multiple homicide incident in which three or more victims are murdered with firearms, within one event, and in one or more locations in close proximity"—have grown in frequency, most school shootings are more like the one that took place at Great Mills High School in which the armed assailant knew the individual he shot (they had a prior romantic relationship).[1]

Brad Bushman, a researcher who has conducted a national study of school shootings, has found important differences between mass shootings and what might be characterized as interpersonal violence involving guns.[2] Bushman finds that whereas nearly all mass school shootings are perpetrated by students who are white and middle class and occur in rural or suburban communities (like Parkland where Stoneman Douglas is located), shooters in urban schools are more often black or Latinx and poor, and typically, they are acquainted with those they shoot. In urban contexts, shooters often have prior arrest records and use handguns that they obtained illegally. In contrast, mass school shooters usually have multiple weapons, including semiautomatic or automatic rifles, which were purchased legally and often obtained from family members. Adding another important distinction, Bushman writes: "Urban shooters don't want anyone to know what they did—they want to hide. Mass shooters want everyone to know."[3]

If we are serious about devising and implementing effective strategies to deter future shootings, we must first be clear about the nature of the problem we are trying to solve. The strategies used to deter mass shootings in rural and suburban communities must be very different than those used to deter violence in urban settings.

In a comprehensive study of mass shootings, University of Massachusetts sociologist Katherine Newman and her colleagues utilized qualitative and quantitative research to identify patterns related to several incidents. Their work shows a consistent link between bullying, alienation, and access to guns as key common variables.[4]

Solid empirical research and common sense rather than fear should serve as the basis for school safety policy. However, careful analysis of the problem is difficult to carry out in an atmosphere of pervasive fear and anxiety. While fear may not be an irrational response to a problem like this one, we must also recognize that fear almost always impairs our ability to think rationally about a problem. In fact, if fear supersedes reason it may actually exacerbate the problem. For example, while arming teachers may seem like one way to deter a shooter, as soon as one considers the numerous ways in which such a strategy could backfire, it may not seem like a wise approach to ensuring student safety.[5] Undoubtedly this is one of the reasons why most law enforcement officials uniformly oppose the idea.

Yet, if arming teachers is not a sound idea that's worthy of being embraced, it is reasonable to ask: What should we do? What are some other ways to promote safety that do not involve increasing the presence of guns and armed personnel and turning schools into facilities that resemble prisons?

Beyond Fear: Trust as a Resource in School Safety

Before offering another set of strategies to deter gun violence in schools, it might be helpful to consider how another problem that generated considerable fear was solved: the pandemic created by the spread of Ebola.

In the summer and fall of 2014, there was an outbreak of Ebola in three West African nations: Liberia, Sierra Leone, and Guinea. With the number of cases increasing rapidly, the Ebola outbreak was soon characterized by the media as a pandemic of "epic proportions."[6] By September of 2014 the World Health Organization projected that the disease would quickly spread beyond the borders of the three West African nations and begin showing up in countries throughout the world. At the time, it was expected that there could be one million cases of Ebola in a mere three months.

Panic set in as health workers returning from the frontlines of fighting the disease contracted the illness themselves, and fears that it would quickly spread to others proliferated. In response, some public officials began calling for visitors from the three West African nations to be quarantined or banned from entering the United States entirely. New Jersey's governor Chris Christie called for an American health worker who had just returned from the region to be quarantined in a tent near Newark international airport.[7]

But less than a year after the disease emerged it was contained. By the fall of 2015 no new cases were recorded in any of the three countries where the outbreak had occurred, and victory over Ebola was officially declared. How was this deadly disease contained—especially given that there still is no vaccine to cure the disease or inoculate people against it? And what can we learn from this success story?

The story of how Ebola came to be contained, without the development of a vaccine, provides an important lesson on how we might overcome our fear to address a pressing, complex problem like gun violence in schools. While politicians like Governor Chris Christie and members of the U.S. Congress called for quarantines, dozens of health workers chose to risk their health and safety, and voluntarily went to the countries most affected by the disease to address the crisis.[8] One of these individuals was Mosoka Fallah, an epidemiologist at MIT. Dr. Fallah, a Liberian who grew up in the poor neighborhood known as West Point in Monrovia, the capital of Liberia and at one point an epicenter of the Ebola outbreak, worked in concert with community activists to combat the disease. Together with other health workers from organizations such as Doctors Without Borders, Dr. Fallah and several health workers launched a massive education campaign on how to care for the sick and the dead, and created a rudimentary public health system where previously none existed. Describing the approach used to counter the spread of the disease, Fallah explained: "If people don't *trust* you they can hide a body and you will never know and Ebola will keep spreading. They've got to *trust* you . . . we don't have the luxury of time."[9]

If trust and education can be used as resources to stop the spread of a deadly disease, can similar strategies be used to address the threat of gun violence in schools? Could a tailored, on-the-ground effort that not only builds trust but seeks answers/solutions with and by the people closest to the problem be effective in making schools safer?

The idea that trust could serve as a resource for making schools safer is a question I took up while doing research at a middle school in Oakland, California, several years ago. The school had been plagued by fights and violence between students, and educators at the school were at a loss about what to do to reduce violence.

Over the course of the next few weeks I conducted interviews with dozens of middle school students and what I learned surprised me. Students were very concerned about their safety but uniformly believed that adults were not able to do anything to protect them. They were far more concerned about being labeled a snitch if they told an adult about impending violence, and reluctantly accepted the idea that dealing with violence through violence, or simply accepting violence as a fact of life, was the only way to address the problem. However, the students also shared that if they had some assurance that teachers would address the threat of violence without revealing the source that had informed them it might occur, they would be willing to speak to adults. One student shared: "If they can show us that we can trust them, then a lot of kids would speak up. Nobody wants to be a victim, and nobody wants to be a snitch either."[10]

This message from middle school students is surprisingly reinforced by findings from research carried out by the U.S. Secret Service.[11] In an effort to find solutions to the threat of mass shootings at schools, the Secret Service has conducted its own research and arrived at recommendations based on the following set of findings, summarized here:

1. **Incidents of targeted violence at school rarely were sudden, impulsive acts.** Most attackers progressed through a process that started with an idea, developed into a plan, led to accessing weapons, and ended with the attack. If the precipitating events had been noticed, the process might have been interrupted before the attack.

2. **Prior to most incidents, other people were often aware of the attacker's idea and/or plan to attack.** A vast body of research shows that when schools develop a culture that promotes trust, and when students have access to counselors and teachers who check in with them on a regular basis, they are more likely to share concerns about their peers with adult educators. As I found in my own research on school safety measures that have averted a shooting, educators who are able to establish trust in their relationships with students can play a role in preventing violence.[12] With trust in place, information related to threats is more likely to be forthcoming. The notion of "snitching" has to be reframed as being responsible about promoting safety. In the case of the Parkland shooting, multiple people did come forward with concerns about the shooter, but officials decided that the shooter couldn't be jailed preemptively, or forced to receive psychological services. However, had counselors been assigned to work with the shooter there is a possibility that the attack might have been prevented.

3. **Most attackers engaged in some behavior prior to the incident that caused others to be concerned or**

indicated a need for help. Some of these behaviors included talking about bringing a gun to school, or warning friends to avoid a certain area of the school on a given day. The Parkland shooter had a history of violent and aggressive behavior, including Instagram posts about becoming a "professional school shooter." Similar threats and warning signs have been acknowledged at other schools that have experienced mass shootings, including at Columbine High School in Littleton, Colorado.

4. **A profile of students who have engaged in targeted school violence in the past is emerging.** Three-quarters of past attackers have been white; one-quarter of the attackers came from other racial and ethnic backgrounds, including African American (12 percent), Hispanic (5 percent), Native Alaskan (2 percent), Native American (2 percent), and Asian (2 percent). Most came from intact families, were doing well in school, and were not loners, according to the report.

5. **Most attackers had experienced significant losses or personal failures and many had difficulty coping with these events. Moreover, many had considered or attempted suicide.** Knowing all students and providing access to counselors who can help them cope with Adverse Childhood Experiences (ACE) in a timely manner is essential to any prevention strategy. At age five, the Parkland shooter witnessed his father die of a heart attack, and his adoptive mother died of pneumonia just three months prior to his deadly attack.

6. **Many attackers felt bullied, persecuted, or injured by others prior to the attack.** Almost two-thirds of shooters reported being targeted by others prior to the attack. Some claim to have experienced severe bullying for a long time. There is evidence that the shooter at Parkland was often mocked for his odd behavior.

The findings generated by the Secret Service mirror findings by Katherine Newman and her colleagues.[13] They suggest that trust and support may in fact serve as an effective way to deter gun violence in schools. Of course, there is no guarantee that providing access to more school counselors and developing support systems for students will prevent another mass shooting or reduce gun violence at schools. The sad truth is that guns are so prevalent and pervasive in American society, there is no way to make schools, churches, airports, army bases, shopping malls, or movie theaters absolutely safe.

However, this does not mean that there we can't take action. In the early 1990s, I worked closely with a middle school in West Oakland that had a reputation for fights and violence. During the middle of the year, one of the school's two security guards was reassigned and a search for a replacement commenced. After the school's principal, Rosalyn Upshaw, met with her faculty, she decided to offer the job to a sixty-three-year-old grandmother who had previously worked at the school as a parent liaison. Given that most school security officers are large men, I asked Ms. Upshaw to explain her decision. She offered the following: "We chose Ms. Maze because we knew that she knew our kids. She can break up any fight or handle any disruption, from a student or an adult, because she is respected. Those are the kinds of adults our kids need."[14]

While there is no guarantee that hiring caring adults will make schools safe, we must recognize that there are alternatives to arming teachers and thereby increasing the presence of guns in schools. Although it has not received the recognition it deserves, trust between students and educators is a valuable resource that can be deployed to help make schools safer than they are now. This is not a new idea. It is as old as the *social contract*; an idea that is fundamental to all democracies. Reinvigorating this ideal and the civic culture that calls upon us to look out for each other may in fact be the best resource we have for countering the threat of gun violence.

Notes

1. William J. Krouse and Daniel J. Richardon, "Mass Murder with Firearms: Incidents and Victims, 1999–2013," Congressional Research Service, July 30, 2015.

2. Brad Bushman, "Narcissism, Fame Seeking and Mass Shootings," *American Behavioral Scientist* 62, no. 2 (2018): 229–41.

3. Bushman, "Narcissism," 28.

4. Kathleen Newman, Cybelle Fox, David Harding, Jal Mehta, and Wendy Roth, *Rampage: The Social Roots of School Shootings* (New York: Basic Books: 2005).

5. M. Hennessy-Fiske, "Dallas Police Chief: Open Carry Makes Things Confusing During Mass Shootings," *Los Angeles Times*, July 11, 2016.

6. For examples of articles warning of the threat posed by Ebola, see "Why Ebola Is so Dangerous," BBC News, October 8, 2014, bbc.com/news/world -africa-26835233, and "Are We Ready for a Global Pandemic of Ebola Virus," in *International Journal of Infectious Diseases* 28 (November 2014): 217–218.

7. Sara Fischer, "Christie's Office: Quarantined Woman Headed to Maine," CNN.com, October 27, 2014, cnn.com/2014/10/26/politics/ebola-quarantine -christie-white-house/index.html.

8. Fischer, "Christie's Office: Quarantined Woman."

9. For a detailed discussion on the strategy employed by Dr. Fallah and others in fighting Ebola in Liberia, see "Back to the Slums of His Youth, to Defuse the Ebola Time Bomb" by Norimitsu Onishi in the *New York Times*, September 14, 2016.

10. Pedro Noguera, *City Schools and the American Dream: Reclaiming the Promise of Public Education* (New York: Teachers College Press, reprint edition, 2003), 125.

11. United States Secret Service and United States Department of Education, *The Final Report and Findings of the Safe School Initiative: Implications for the Prevention of School Attacks in the United States*, Washington, DC, July 2004.

12. A. Wade Boykin and Pedro Noguera, *Creating the Opportunity to Learn: Moving from Research to Practice to Close the Achievement Gap* (Virginia: ASCD, 2011).

13. Newman et al., *Rampage*.

14. Noguera, *City Schools and the American Dream*.

How Hurricane Harvey Altered My Perspective as a Teacher

Jeff Collier

Jeff Collier teaches band and music and currently serves as a band director for La Porte Independent School District's sixth-grade campus in La Porte, Texas. He is pursuing a doctorate in professional leadership from the University of Houston.

I CURRENTLY HAVE THE UNIQUE EXPERIENCE OF BEING BOTH A TEACHER and a student. As a middle-school band director by day and a doctoral student by night, I find that the opportunity to teach while taking classes can often be a juggling act. I have always enjoyed being a student, but I also have had very few roadblocks standing in my way; I grew up in a supportive family that encouraged me to get good grades, stay out of trouble, and complete my homework. While I've always known that some of my students experienced difficulties outside the classroom that prevented them from paying attention, I don't think I ever truly understood why a student would lack the motivation to be successful. Until two months ago, that is.

When Hurricane Harvey struck in August 2017, my wife, pets, and I were forced to evacuate our house by boat. We ended up losing our home, cars, and most of our possessions. Despite being safe and taking comfort from the support of friends and fellow teachers, the experience changed me as a student.

For the first time, I had mental roadblocks. When I would sit down to read, I could not comprehend the words on the page. When

I attempted to type a paper, I could not find the motivation to complete the project. My mind would instantly drift to the issues we were facing and to flashbacks of the disaster that we went through. This was the case despite the fact that earning a doctorate is something I have aspired to achieve for years.

A Better Understanding

As I lay awake at night, I drew connections between my current situation and the issues many students experience, not just the impacts of the flood—that was now the easy part to comprehend—but other roadblocks that are less easy to see. Apart from natural disaster, poverty, racism, depression, bullying, divorce, and other complex issues weigh heavily on many students' minds. These roadblocks are especially hard to address when they are not readily apparent to others.

Throughout my entire teaching career, I never really understood how students could sit in class and do nothing when given time to practice, or decline to participate, or refuse to turn in a homework assignment—even when they were given several opportunities. It was not until Hurricane Harvey that I got a glimpse of the mentality of struggling students. I can think back on how I would tell students to be better and work harder, thinking that they were simply being lazy or entitled.

I used to believe that if we helped students with external factors—giving them food, providing transportation, giving them after-school library access, or providing them with a safe and comfortable learning environment—that the pathway to learning would open and the issues weighing on their minds would magically disappear. I now know this is far from the case. I can't imagine feeling the way I felt after Harvey and being asked to concentrate or to learn a topic in which I had no interest.

The Life Preserver Students Need

Support does help facilitate learning, to some extent. In my own experience, I know that if I did not have a loving wife, professors working with me, fellow classmates encouraging me, or friends to stay with, I would have dropped out of my academic program. Thanks to a strong support system, I feel that I can continue psychologically to tread water while wearing a life preserver until I am mentally ready to swim. At the very least, this network has prevented me from sinking.

This is why, since the storm, I have put even more of an emphasis on building relationships with my students. I pass out questionnaires to get to know them better and have been to football games and piano recitals to show them that I genuinely care about them and their interests. I want to show students that they are a part of something bigger than themselves and that they have people who will support them, even when they can't be on task.

I am also more mindful about looking for situations that may be impacting my students, and try to consistently remind them that I care about them and believe in them. I am more sympathetic and patient with students who are struggling, and I have learned not to take students' apathetic attitudes personally.

It is critical for teachers to give students the gift of grace, as well as tools to surmount the mental roadblocks described above. Even when it feels like your support is not making a difference, it could very well be the only life preserver that a student is holding on to.

I Was Raised to Believe Education Could Keep Me Safe

fredrick scott salyers

*fredrick scott salyers is an educator, writer, and photographer who serves
as the dean of student culture and college readiness at a high school in
the Crown Heights neighborhood of Brooklyn, New York. He is also
a creative consultant for Langston League, a nonprofit that educates
middle school boys on cultural self-awareness and creative writing.*

I WORRY A LOT ABOUT THE STUDENTS IN THE HIGH SCHOOL WHERE I
teach. One, in particular, is bright but struggles in class. He rarely
ever smiles and he acts out, going so far recently as to threaten another
teacher. As a black male teacher—one of too few in the profession—I
feel especially compelled to help this young black man reach his potential. Part of that work is teaching him the dangers that might exist
for him, including the police.

The killing of Texas teenager Jordan Edwards proves, though,
that it's not just black boys with behavior issues who are in danger.
Jordan—a high school freshman, star athlete, and honor student—
was shot dead by a police officer on April 29, 2017, while leaving a
house party. As he rode away from the party in a car driven by his
older brother, officers who'd been called to the scene fired multiple
rifle rounds at the car. One bullet went through the passenger window, striking Jordan in the head. Murder charges were since filed

against the officer who fired the fatal shot.[1] In 2018, he was convicted and sentenced to fifteen years in prison.

It's a near impossible task to educate black children in a society that constantly interrupts that work with such violence. Still, it's incumbent on educators like us to guide our students through the moment we're living in—even when we can't answer all their questions, and even if we're sometimes confused ourselves.

I began teaching in 2014, the year when the police killings of Eric Garner, Michael Brown, and Tamir Rice dominated headlines. The tragedies have since piled on, a new one seeming to occur every month since I first stepped into a classroom. I currently teach ninth-graders at a predominantly black charter school in Brooklyn, and I often find myself struggling to make sense of these events for my students.

I've shown them clips from popular films like *Selma* and *Fruitvale Station* and prepared lessons on the civil rights movement, and I've done my best to ground it all in the subjects I was hired to teach—American history, composition, and college readiness. My hope is that these films will encourage my students to connect today's police violence to our nation's history of racial injustice. And, because there are no easy answers, that they'll be encouraged by the perseverance of those who came before them.

I can't help but worry that I'm sending them mixed messages, however; teaching them lessons on resistance while also policing their conduct day to day. As an administrator and one of just a few black male teachers in my school, I'm often charged with disciplining students. I find myself offering similar guidance to many of them: "get good grades," "respect authority," "keep your nose clean." It's instruction and advice that can feel pointless when a "good kid" like Jordan Edwards can have his life cut short by those sworn to serve and protect him. Still, I try in hopes that good grades and polite behavior will insulate my students from some of society's dangers, if not all of them.

The Monday after the police killed Edwards, I asked the students in my college readiness class to watch a newsclip about the shooting and write out their feelings, or sit in silence and reflect. Many of them were already aware of what happened. I was proud that so many of them were abreast of the news but saddened by their reflections. At just fourteen and fifteen years old, many of them have already come to accept deaths like Jordan's as the norm, and readily expect that any one of them could be next. "Will this police officer even be fired?" one asked. "Was the cop white?"

The young man I worry about the most was more talkative than usual that day. During the class discussion, he shared his guilt about being the only one of his friends who "made it"—making it meaning still being alive, and free. The guilt sometimes cripples him, he said, and high-profile police killings like Jordan's compound that guilt with a feeling of hopelessness. They make him think he will die in the streets one way or another.

I didn't know what to say then and I still don't have a response for him. I've always taught students that earning an education might have the power to exempt them from the perils of being black in America, or at least give them a chance at something more. I was raised on that notion and believed it so much that I became an educator. But deaths like Jordan's leave me choking on the reality that nothing I can teach will shield my students from becoming the next hashtag.

In lieu of protection, I offer what I can. I provide a space for my students to express their feelings. I offer love and consideration in our day-to-day interactions and do my best to make them feel seen and, hopefully, safe for a few hours each day.

Notes

1. Adeel Hassan, "Family of Jordan Edwards Says 15 Years Is Not Enough for Officer Who Murdered Him," *New York Times*, August 31, 2018.

Calling on Omar

Carla Shalaby

*Carla Shalaby, a former elementary school teacher and director of elementary
education programs at Brown University and Wellesley College, is a research
scholar based in Detroit committed to education as the practice of freedom.
She is the coordinator of social justice initiatives and community internships
at the University of Michigan School of Education and the author of*
Troublemakers: Lessons in Freedom from Young Children at School.

"CIRCLE UP," THE KINDERGARTEN TEACHER SAYS WITH AN INVITING
voice. "It's time for math."

Solidly trained in their routines, the children start to gather, taking
their assigned spots on the rug. Both friends and foes have been sep-
arated by the careful engineering of these rug-spot assignments. This
is math time. Not the time for silly fun-making between friends or for
elbow jostling between enemies. It's a small space to share and these
five-year-old bodies are bouncy and wriggling, but for the most part,
contained. Under control.

I'm in the classroom to visit a student teacher, and together we're
witnessing the model of this mentor teacher. "After math it will be
time for recess, and I have to give you some special instructions." The
bodies become still, listening. She continues. "As you know, Darell
has been out for several weeks, healing from his hip surgery." All
eyes turn sympathetically to Darell, who is shifting his body under
the weight of this attention. "We have to be extra gentle so that we
don't hurt his hip. This is especially true at recess, when things can

get rough. We can't be rough with Darell. We have to keep his hip safe."

Half the little hands go up. There are *lots* of questions and comments and curiosities.

The teacher waves their hands down with her single, authoritative hand. "Not now. This isn't a discussion." She is warm, but stern. The majority of little hands go down, save for one. Omar's hand remains. And it is a waving hand now, pulsing with the urgency of whatever he needs to say.

The teacher attempts to start the math lesson, but Omar won't abandon his desire. "Miss," he begins to call out. "I just wanted to—"

She interrupts. "Omar, this is a time for my voice, not yours. We are already late beginning math, and we need to move on so you're not late for recess. You don't want to miss recess, right?" I can't tell if this last part is a question or a threat. But her tone is now more stern than warm. Omar puts his hand down. His shoulders sink a little.

We watch the math lesson for forty minutes. I'm bored. Omar contributes only when forced. The lesson wraps up and the children are just about to leave the circle to get ready for recess. Omar calls out, "Wait!" He is loud enough to be heard over the ensuing chaos of transition. Everyone stops to listen. "I just wanted to say that I'm glad Darell is back."

Darell smiles shyly.

The children clap for him, celebrating—for just a brief, human moment—his long-awaited return to their community.

What lesson did the teacher deliver that day?

What did Omar teach?

Everything I know about what it means to be human, I learned from kindergartners. When we become distracted by what *we* think is important, young children redirect our focus, centering on the need to be human together. They are blessed with a lack of self-restraint, and abandoning the pretense of politeness, they center their own interests, their own questions, their own desires, over and above the imposed agenda of adults. In this way, they remind us that they are in charge. What might they teach us, if we allowed ourselves to learn from them in school?

School is a place where a sense of urgency abounds. Time is an acutely limited resource; teachers have *so* very much to do, and never enough time to do it. By waving those little hands down, the teacher taught the children that her lesson plan was more important than their curiosities. By insisting on her voice over Omar's, the teacher reinforced the authority of adults over children. These are normal-ized lessons in school, where time is limited and priorities required, and because we believe that we know what is best for children, we take for granted that they should defer to the wisdom of our expe-rience and accept our authority. I understood this teacher's urgent desire to begin the math lesson. That urgency felt familiar to me as an educator.

But I'm learning to better understand, and to learn from, Omar's equally urgent desire to prioritize the need for being human together in school. His insistence on interrupting the teacher's lesson to in-stead offer his own reminded me of the power of children, and of the need to remember myself as a human being first, and an educa-tor second. They correct us when we misstep—when we forget. They remind us what school is actually for, what we are really there to do and to teach and to become together. We are at school to learn what it means to be human: to protect each other, to insist on community, to keep both hips *and* hearts safe. While the teacher worried about not hurting Darell, Omar worried about modeling gentleness more broadly, more universally, more collectively. How might we emulate this shift in our own model as educators and as human beings?

The lessons we choose to prioritize in school are largely driven by what we assume children need by way of preparation for the world. But who among us can look at the world we have now and respon-sibly argue that we should use our sacred time in schools to prepare children for the world as is? This is not the time to teach children how to be in the world as is. This is a time to invite them to imagine the world we want, and then to figure out and practice who we will all need to become.

Dreaming up a new world—a more humane world—requires the work of our children. Age is a disadvantage when it comes to imagination. Our longer-lived experience in the world as is constrains our capacity to imagine the world as it could be, as it should be, as it must be.

These times—like many urgent, painful times before—call on us to draw on every possible resource in our struggle to make schools safe. But I fear that we too often overlook our most valuable resource in that struggle: the children. We need to call on them. We can learn to thoughtfully abandon our desire to protect kids, to control and constrain them, and to instead recognize in them the desire to actively participate in the shared human responsibility to keep each other safe, in reciprocity and in community.

It's time to circle up with our children. To take up the spots we assign to ourselves and to each other, and to figure out—in classrooms and beyond them—what it means to be in community, what it means to protect each other, and what it means to be human.

School Justice:
Teaching Politically Fraught Topics

T. Elijah Hawkes

T. Elijah Hawkes is the principal at Randolph Union High School in Randolph, Vermont. He was the founding principal of the James Baldwin School in New York City, and his writings about adolescence, public school, and democracy have appeared in the Huffington Post, Education Week, Kappan, *and in two books published by Rethinking Schools:* The New Teacher Book *and* Rethinking Sexism, Gender, and Sexuality.

YOU ARE A TEACHER TROUBLED BY THE PARADOX. YOU BELIEVE IN THE creative and liberating power of education, and yet you work in a system that has perfected regimentation and confinement. You know the health and rejuvenation of your society demands disruptive and youthful critique, and yet your classroom and school can stand only so much youthful disruption. You strive to empower young people to challenge the status quo, and yet getting through any given day demands that you demand that rules as they are be followed.

And the paradox is more troubling still: you believe your school can be a place where youth learn the names and ways of oppressors— indeed how to unseat them—and yet you know the schoolhouse is but a few steps from the master's house, and your tools are also his tools, and you are an agent of his state, a nation born and built through genocide and slavery.

In particular, the school discipline system troubles you. You see how it punishes young people, how it makes them feel, and how it mirrors the brutal racial and socioeconomic biases of the criminal justice system. You see how schools rank and sort according to how people all across the land are unjustly ranked and sorted. You see who gets suspended and who doesn't, and who gets suspended again, and who doesn't come back. You know the school-to-prison pipeline is real.

What can a teacher do about this? You could be forgiven for an inclination to complacency. But true engagement of the paradox is a struggle, and struggle conjures hope. When our curriculum and pedagogy are committed to the struggle, our day-to-day work can inspire hope and be a driver of substantive reform.

A Restorative Justice Class

I'm a school principal, but every couple of years I teach a class. Recently I was co-teacher of a class focused on restorative justice. It was a year-long elective for high school students, grades 9–12, structured around an essential question: do schools and courts treat people fairly? The school's own discipline code and punitive practices were the subject of our learning and work, as was the criminal justice system that intersects with the lives of our students and families outside of school. As a member of the school community with substantial positional power, for me to engage with students in a study of how my power is wielded—often in ways that can feel punishing or disempowering to others—was a way for me to both walk in the paradox and wrestle it. Any teacher with the power to include or exclude, confine, hold back, or hold after can engage these very same questions and become one who both holds the master's tools and interrogates what they build and how. This was the description of the class in the course catalogue:

> Do schools in our state discipline students fairly? Do students with certain identities get suspended more often than others? Does a school suspension have any connection to dropping out? Does dropping out of school have any correlation to getting

into trouble with the law? And what about our legal system: Do the courts treat people fairly? Does VT have too many prisons or not enough? Should people with mental health challenges go to jail if they commit a crime? How should people with opiate addiction be treated when in custody?

As a teacher and principal, I've worked in city schools, and rural and small-town schools. The school where I taught this class is a grade 7–12 public school serving three central Vermont towns. The poverty rates have nearly doubled in the elementary schools in the last decade and nearly everyone knows someone who has a friend or family member troubled by addiction to opiates. More than 95 percent of students in the school are white, but the student population embodies an important heterogeneity in terms of family background and parent profession.

The students in the class were a diverse group in terms of socioeconomic class and family experience, including a girl with a sister in prison, a boy with a dad in the police force, a boy with the tumult of substance abuse at home, a girl who struggles with depression, other students from families stable and unstable, others whose stories I hardly know. They did good and important work together.

Three years since, the course is still running, now taught by other faculty. Our school's discipline procedures have been revised to include restorative process; we've begun to reduce our mandatory-minimum suspension sentences through the use of restorative practice; student facilitators still do much of the work, building on the strong foundation laid by students in the first year.

As a white, middle-class man with ample privilege, I hope I'm not deluding myself when I think this class represents a successful effort to retool the master's tools. Those tools and resources, when it comes to the schoolhouse, include teacher time, teacher pay, student time, and the power-tools used to frame the discourse, ask questions, and hold the mic. If a school can allocate those resources to deconstruct habits and ways that devalue and disempower people, then the troubling paradox becomes somewhat less troubling.

Lessons Taught and Lessons Learned

Though I taught this class at a school in small-town Vermont, the lessons we wrote and learned, and the school-reform work the students put in motion can translate to any school setting where there is a teacher ready to engage students in a study of criminal justice and school justice, including the school's own systems for sorting, disciplining, exiling, and confining.

Our goal was to reform the school's disciplinary system and how our own school functions in the larger school-to-prison pipeline—and I think we made some progress. Here are eight important characteristics of the work:

1. Make the extra-curricular curricular.

The first important step in the development of this class was that we took what might have been the work of an after-school or lunch-time committee and we figured out how to fold it into the school day.

After school is often when special initiatives reside, get their start—or try to get started. It's when service learning groups, the gay-straight alliance, a student government body, or the climate change club will meet. After school may also be when educators and students might try to organize the work of restorative justice or peer mediation. But after-school hours can limit the scope of the work. If a school can integrate restorative justice work into the school day, that group and its mission are suddenly accorded multiple hours of time each week, and given the benefit of dedicated teacher time and other resources accorded to school-day classes. Our restorative justice class had more than three hours each week to pursue the goals and essential questions of our work.

2. Ask a big question.

A good essential question is one that has more than one answer and has moral, ethical, personal, and/or political dimensions. "Do our schools and courts treat people fairly?" was the essential question of this class and it is a tent-of-a-question, big enough to hold everyone's identity and experience, however congruent or divergent, and in ways that have personal, political, moral, and ethical points of entry.

I've made the mistake of trying to invite an ideologically diverse group of people to the table while not crafting my questions or topics carefully enough to make all feel welcome. I once organized a conference for educators and professionals from other circles. I emailed a group of friends—some on the political left, others on the right—to ask them to spread the word. The purpose of the conference was to consider the challenges schools face when tackling important contemporary problems, such as "wage stagnation, youth flight, climate crisis, gun violence, opiate addiction, terrorism and war, child poverty, racial and class divisions . . ." I thought this was an ideologically neutral list of topics, but I got some responses filled with great frustration, suggesting that I was promoting the "co-opting" of children. I was surprised, but then tried to learn from the response. What if my topics list had included "gun rights and gun control" instead of just "gun violence" or "minimum-wage laws" instead of "wage stagnation"? I think people of more diverse political leanings would have been interested in joining the discussion.

For this reason, when framing the questions for this class, I left out "police brutality"—though it was my intention and responsibility to introduce this topic to our work once it was underway. But I wanted students to be drawn to the course who have a favorable view of law enforcement, just as I wanted those who might be critical of how state power is wielded. I also left the word "teachers" out of the essential question. "Do teachers treat students fairly?" might have made many of my colleagues defensive or worried about the work of the class, rather than open to the proposals the students would produce. Indeed, by asking "Do our schools treat people fairly?" I implicated myself as a potential subject of critique and questioning, modeling a posture I hoped the broader community would also adopt.

3. Involve people with positional power.
For many reasons, the success of our school's inquiry into criminal justice, restorative justice, and school justice was linked to the

involvement of the principal, me. I was a co-teacher of the class; my colleague was a first-year, long-term substitute social studies teacher. He was an important partner, but the course was one I had framed and decided to offer.

If there were to be any changes to our school's practice, the students would have to discover the rationale themselves and persuade the faculty to support their proposal. But my role as an administrator helped the students gain access to precious time at faculty meetings, and later helped the students craft an experimental program of youth-led restorative practice, where questions of confidentiality or parental involvement can benefit from the perspective of an administrator. It was also about giving cover: if something went wrong when the students were in change of facilitation and parents or community members raised concerns, I wanted to be able to shield the kids from blame.

There are a number of ways to incorporate substantive administrative involvement. Administrators could be part of an advisory board to the course, consulting on important questions, and serving as an authentic audience to evaluate the work. Or, school administrators could visit the course as guests or presenters of information, ideas, perspectives, and history. Whatever their involvement, it is important that the adults whose job descriptions involve apportioning consequences for breaking rules be involved in a class that is about the school's own justice system.

4. Establish trust.

In any class that endeavors to get personal or get political, it is essential to establish trust in the first days, weeks, and months. The children must trust that crucial needs will be met by the adult caregivers. Each child must come to believe that the adults are trustworthy and that the child, him- or herself, is worthy of protection and nourishment.

The positional authority of the adults in the room—the teachers— is an essential ingredient here. The careful use of authority should not be confused with authoritarianism, and it should be clearly established up front that the positional power in the room will be used to enable the powerful voices of others.

All of this happens in the trust-building period, the first weeks or months of the class. Group work should wait until the teacher has established a whole-class format of interaction. This can take some time and should not be rushed. The whole-class format should occur in a circle or square or U shape, some shape that allows the adults to see the faces of every student in the room, and invites students to see and interact with each other as much as with the adults. The adults must demonstrate that breaches of the norms established by the group will not be tolerated, and that voices that take risks will be heard and never ridiculed. Students should not be divided into self-governing groups until the norms of whole-group governance have been established with the teacher: an authority can't be delegated and distributed unless it exists.

This is not to say that inquiry-based instruction isn't essential here. Norms, for instance, can be developed in collaboration with the class. A teacher should know in what direction, however, this process needs to lead. Some useful norms to help establish trust in the classroom can be:

- **One mic, or don't talk when others are talking.** This may be the Golden Rule. It should be followed in any classroom that wants to evoke personal expression. To ensure that every voice is heard is to value every voice.
- **Avoid absolutes.** It is all too easy to alienate someone or some group of people when we casually use absolutes like "all," "always," "every," etc. Making generalizations, using words like "most" or "often," is safer.
- **Use "I" statements.** Speak from your own personal truth and personal experience. Also, acknowledge the "I" statements of others.

After establishing norms, it is important to create forums for discussion expansive with personal, political, moral, and ethical dimensions. But, you don't need to start out talking to each other directly about each other. Discussing literature, stories, and films can give the class an opportunity to practice using its norms to build vocabulary for discussing sensitive content and help establish a trust-containing and trustworthy space.

The stories we read should, indeed, raise questions that have no easy answers. The literature or films we choose to help us pursue the essential questions of the course and build our skills in talking about complicated personal and political questions shouldn't be complex. Simple, short, and open-ended is best, for these stories leave room for the students of the class to explore who they are and what they believe, revealing who they are through connections to the story in a way that can be personal or not, depending on their readiness for confessional sharing. The teacher's role is to ensure norms are followed, trust is built, and mature vocabulary for discussing personal and political topics is developed.

5. *Engage in inquiry.*

Students kept journals and were asked to do an entry every one or two weeks. The third journal prompt for the course asked the students to refer to the course description and consider: "Which of the essential questions of the course seems most important to *you*? Why is this question important to you, or our community? And do you know of resources/texts/people/films that can help us investigate this question?"

Linda was a junior, a thoughtful observer of the world, hesitant and wandering and creative in her verbal expression. Born into an immigrant family from Eastern Europe, she came to school for a partial program and was homeschooled for her other subjects. In response to our prompt about which questions she was most interested in exploring, she focused on a topic that had come up in the early weeks of the class, recidivism and reintegration of people into their communities after spending time incarcerated:

I am especially interested in resettlement programs because it's maybe something our class could come back to pretty easily and be involved in in a profound way. I'm also just really interested in it, there's something intriguing to me about the mental process that these people have to go through, and the way that communities respond to their integration.

I'm also interested in a topic that Alice brought up about prison life in general, and I think that's something that kind of connects to resettlement programs in an important way. Like, what is that change like for them psychologically? They are coming from a very hard place, and they might be expecting the same world when they come out, but things usually have changed pretty drastically.

Another student, Nelson, a senior, wrote about his interest in "the pipeline between the school and prison":

Mostly how the school creates a segregation between students who will go on to college and those who will not and how the school does this and makes these kids left behind and how this creates the school to prison pipeline.

Another way is to look at certain statistics at schools like suspensions to imprisonment or expulsion or grades or maybe even tardies to what happens to these kids who have a lot of these after high school.

Another way of looking at this topic that I would be interested in is if the justice system inside of schools works and is fair for all students. You could correlate this topic with the one before or even just focus in on this topic. I think this topic would be beneficial to our classroom and our school itself to know. I think you could look at statistics of the justice system of the school's by looking at the rules of schools and compare them to ours and statistics of expulsion, suspension (in or out of school), and what the suspensions and expulsions are for and if the graduation rate has something to do with how many of these the schools gives out and how well our school does compared to other schools.

We asked each student to turn their interests into a research project and mini-lesson through which they would teach the class what they'd learned. We developed a rubric together to evaluate the project. The other teacher and I modeled the research and lessons. I chose to do a presentation on white-collar crime, because there was much in the local news about it at the time, and there was a seminar at a nearby college on the topic that we were planning to attend. My colleague did his research and mini-lesson on the "war on drugs," integrating resources we would return to later in the class: Michelle Alexander's book, *The New Jim Crow*, and Ava DuVernay's film, *13th*.

Nelson's presentation was particularly formative in the evolution of the class. He reached out to the American Civil Liberties Union of Vermont and acquired data that demonstrated correlations between special education status, drop-out rates, and the state's prison population, which was valuable information that other students would later use in their efforts to persuade the faculty that restorative practice was a necessary but missing ingredient in our disciplinary interventions.

In their end-of-semester reflections, students expressed appreciation for the way that these individual research projects allowed them to educate themselves and their peers. They enjoyed choosing a topic of personal interest, and they appreciated being taught the mini-lessons by their peers. And they felt proud to shape the future path our work would take over the course of the year. Two students, Alice and Karla, went to hear Karla's sister participate in a presentation about women's experiences in prison. This prompted us to visit a correctional facility to tour and better understand what life is like in prison, and students in the class would conduct focus groups about what it's like to be part of the school's disciplinary processes.

6. *Connect with cops and community.*

The core purpose of public schools is to help young people become informed, contributing, critically thinking members of our democracy. But it can be risky for teachers to open conversations about potent political topics, especially those with personal relevance like criminal justice. Students can feel that their values are being challenged—and perhaps they are. And teachers might be accused of bias or indoctrination. So when I teach in ways that get political, I invite many members of the community to share their points of view. This fortifies the classroom and the teacher against accusations of bias, for there are other, non-teacher adults with experience and expertise whose perspectives are part of the work.

Early on in the restorative justice elective we invited members of the town's justice board to class, which included the director of the organization, a police officer, and another community member. Later in the course we heard from the father of one of our students, a state trooper, who was a special guest. Just as it is valuable to integrate school administrators into a course that explores school discipline systems, so too is it valuable to expose students to the perspectives of law enforcement officers in projects that focus on the criminal justice system. Granted, our community's police officers are trusted by most families, educators, and others. When I worked in New York City schools, there were some officers I would have been reluctant to bring into the classroom, given their reputation for brutality toward young people outside of school. But even there, I knew officers and a school safety agent who I trusted to bring into our classroom.

A curriculum focused on school and criminal justice should integrate the school's administration and local law enforcement into the work. This helps assure multiple perspectives, buttress the teacher's pedagogy with the strength of local professionals and leaders, and create allies in the community who can affirm the integrity of the work in the face of any concerns that the school might be co-opting a child into political beliefs not supported in the home.

7. Become informed and qualified.

In my past work as principal of the James Baldwin School in New York City, and in my prior experience as a teacher, I'd gained some skills in facilitating restorative justice interventions. But the students in this class I was teaching did not have such experience. It was important that they develop the knowledge and qualifications needed to help implement the work they intended to do.

After a few months of work, no student was yet an expert, but they were better informed, eager, and ready to convince the faculty that peer mediations and restorative justice circles ought to be more broadly piloted immediately, in light of disconcerting data on school and state discipline systems. By the time the students were making their arguments at the faculty meeting, they had:

- Invited a well-regarded community organizer and practitioner of restorative practice for a day-long training at the school to help them develop their own understanding of the principles and practices of restorative interventions.
- Asked the school's administrative office to provide them with multiple years of discipline data, which is compiled each year for state and federal census reports, and invited the school secretary to come and discuss the data she'd compiled for them.
- Studied the school's data and noticed that, in our 7–12 middle/high school, physical conflicts seemed most prevalent in the middle school years, and then showed a steady decline as students got older. They also noticed that incidents involving tension between student behavior and adult authority seemed to decrease markedly after tenth grade.
- Conducted focus groups with students who'd had school discipline referrals in school in past years—including some of the students in the course. These focus groups revealed that many students felt many of the current interventions were ineffective—largely due to a lack of dialogue and students feeling unheard by the other people involved, typically teachers.
- Conducted a broad student survey to gather further information from more students about the discipline system at the school.
- Educated each other, as noted above, about the school-to-prison pipeline in our state, and the particular disparities involving students with special needs.
- Participated in and then facilitated circle-based conversations, with protocols, prompts and talking pieces refined by them.

When the time came, I felt they were ready—but I warned them that they couldn't assume they would get a positive response from the faculty. I told them of my own vivid memory of being interviewed for the principal position, when I was asked whether I would commit to upholding disciplinary consequences—from warnings and detentions to suspensions and expulsions. The teacher who asked me about my commitment to discipline is still at the school, I told them, and there are many people who understandably feel strong allegiance to our traditional consequences. There are likewise many members of the parent and wider community who feel a tough-on-discipline approach is what is needed in schools.

8. Value the faculty's perspective.

The faculty meeting is a weekly gathering of fifty or so teachers and administration. The students were very nervous to present their case for implementing restorative practices at the school as early as the following semester. But they made a persuasive presentation, followed by small group discussions to ensure every faculty member's voice was heard. There were ample concerns and questions, but no strong objections from the faculty. They had a green light to move forward.

In the week that followed, one of the students wrote in his journal about his work in preparing for the faculty meeting:

I have spent most of my class time in the past two weeks working on the presentation that was for the faculty meeting. We needed to get across to the faculty what restorative justice is, why it is important and what it will look like in our school. I worked on improving the three sections of the presentations so that they are informative without getting into too much detail so we do not bore them or make the meeting confusing.

I decided along with others that showing that the school discipline system we have now creates the school to prison pipeline in Vermont by showing the faculty a graph that I gathered from the Vermont ACLU which showed the Vt school to prison pipeline perfectly and how our discipline system targets specific groups of people and how restorative justice is proven to help end this awful cycle.

Another thing I helped out on was the focus group we had done with students who have gone through discipline at our school and have something to say about it or just want to talk about it. I did not really facilitate but helped to ask questions and listen to the feedback so that I could help bring it together and use for the faculty meeting to also show that students do not really like what we are doing now. We gathered some great quotes and stories from students and teachers which really made me feel as though we are not only doing something very important in our school but that the rest of our community is in support of it too.

As these reflections show, including student and faculty stakeholders in the preparations helped build a sense of collective will for the work. The green light from faculty was especially crucial, not only because it felt good to have adult support, but because teachers directly shape how the school responds to conflicts and broken rules. Every day, teachers passively and actively sanction some behaviors and not others, and they appropriately influence what consequences are apportioned for violations of norms. For the restorative justice class to really get to work, the faculty needed to be willing to participate in mediations with students, and to accept mediations and circle process as consequences for student conflict.

9. See the unconventional successes.

That the students felt the mandate for change from their peers was just as important as gaining support of faculty. They gained this through the focus groups and the study of the school's discipline data. A sense of mandate from other students helped generate will to do work that, for most adolescents, would not be conventionally exciting. The work is often quiet, sometimes slow, and has none of the adrenaline rush of competition. It could easily be labeled boring, and the victories are about careful listening and skillful questions. Sometimes the successes are hard to see.

Success could be as simple as a well-phrased question, or the empathic paraphrasing of someone's feelings. Sometimes the success was about using intuition, going off-script, or not following the protocols we'd developed. Helping the students to see those quiet victories was part of my role.

A conflict between two high school students, Kora and Lila, was one intervention when the success was hard to see. These were troubled girls who could cause trouble. In fact I don't know where either of these students is now. Last I heard of Lila, a school had called us wondering if she was legitimately homeless, as her mom was asserting. I said we didn't know. A few weeks before I got that call, I'd asked the local police to see if they could find her—so I was glad to know she was, to some degree, okay. Last I heard of Kora, she was in a residential placement to better help her with her rage and her self-loathing.

One day last year, before either girl had left us, Kora had come into Lila's classroom and punched her in the face. A suspension for Kora followed, and following that we held a post-suspension re-entry circle. It was the first re-entry circle that students from my restorative justice class helped to facilitate. It wasn't as easy as the peer mediations with younger, middle school students that they'd been conducting. Kora was not receptive to their questions. Kora was not ready to be vulnerable or accept responsibility. Kora was derisive and curt.

Kora was a young woman I'd gotten to know well over the past year, but mostly on the periphery of the conflict she'd cultivated: she would come to me in frustration with a teacher, or I'd hear her cursing at a peer in the hall, or catch her offering a threat. I found ways to redirect her, or help her and the others involved find a superficial solution. But we never got to the root of any issue. I often asked her about talking directly to the person she was angry with. She would invariably reply, "They're not worth it." By which I think she also meant, "Nor am I."

The students in the restorative justice class debriefed the circle. They felt low. There had been no good feelings, no easy resolution or simple next steps charted. I asked a few questions. They said Kora had mentioned being willing to do a mediation with Lila, face-to-face. My own face brightened. "That's a success!" I told them. "I've never been able to get her to agree to talk to anyone she's had conflict with. Good work!"

Conclusion: Sustaining the Work

In the first semester of the class, we focused on understanding the need, defining the work, and making room for it within the school. In the second semester the students conducted mediations to resolve or prevent conflict between students in the middle school, did a few mediations between students and teachers in the high school, and conducted a couple of post-suspension re-entry restorative circles. Cases were referred to the class by me, my co-principal colleague, and by teachers.

By the end of the year they produced a handbook to hand down to the students and teacher who would conduct the class in the following year. It remains a high school elective that's offered to this day, and it helps our disciplinary interventions focus less on punishment and more on healing.

We are now using our restorative circles to reduce the duration of some of the mandatory-minimum suspension sentences associated with certain infractions in our discipline code. For instance, a student who has earned a multiday suspension for illegal substance possession could have that suspension reduced through a successful restorative circle. I look forward to a new cohort of student facilitators, and to how our practice will continue to evolve.

After these first years, it will be important for us to study the school's discipline data, and disaggregate for students with special needs, in particular, since this was one of the school-to-drop-out/ school-to-prison pipelines that our founding students intended to disrupt. The number of students of color in our central Vermont school is miniscule, and so it is difficult to see meaningful trends in annual data for those demographics, but for this reason it is important that the class monitor statewide trends, for bias is certainly visible there and must be interrogated.

The multiyear sustainability of this school reform work is possible largely because we have made a class of it, guided by a teacher and led by a group of students who dedicate hours each week to get the work done. I don't see the work surviving if we don't allot time for it within the normal school day, and so I remain committed to allocating resources with this in mind. It is one small way the master's tools can be used to reform and reshape the rooms and ways of the master's house.

Race
Matters

Don't Say Nothing

Jamilah Pitts

Jamilah Pitts is the dean of students at a high school in Harlem, New York, and a former English teacher. She is also a curriculum developer and a consultant providing anti-racist, culturally responsive workshops for educators.

AS EDUCATORS WE (SOMETIMES UNKNOWINGLY) STEP INTO THE ROLES OF advocate, caretaker, guide, and even mother or father to students. Students pay attention to everything we say and do. They particularly pay attention to our silence.

We may be uncomfortable talking about race, but we can no longer afford to be silent. We have chosen a profession, which—like parenting—requires that our comforts come second to those of children.

Many black and brown students are educated in school systems and classrooms where they, despite making up the racial majority, are taught how to understand the world by a staff comprised of a powerful minority. When their teachers choose to remain silent about moments of racial tension or violence—violence that may well touch students' own communities or families—these children are overtly reminded of their inferior place in society.

Even as a black teacher, I have to set a tone for my students that signals that it's safe to talk about race. Even with me, students of color are afraid to say the word "white" or to name the blatant racism of slavery and Jim Crow. If that's the case, imagine how much more difficult it is for them to engage in dialogue about mass incarceration rates; the militarism of police; the killing of innocent black men and women; cycles of poverty; the destruction of our bodies, minds, and souls; the lack of access to healthy food and quality schools; and gentrification. These are all symptoms of a type of racism that remains deadly to this day because, despite bodies lying in the street, we refuse to talk about it.

White teachers must also broach these topics with white children attending white schools. These students *need* to learn about the destructive power of racism and brutality that have plagued our country for centuries. They should also understand that Alton Sterling, Philando Castile, and Trayvon Martin were preceded in death by Emmett Till, Jimmie Lee Jackson, and countless others whose stories and deaths we must also teach. Our lack of instruction becomes deadly when we allow fear and discomfort to indirectly allow white students to labor under false, privileged assumptions.

Moreover, the silence on the part of white teachers who teach black and brown children is insulting. Imagine seeing white people, the perceived dominant race, loving and appreciating black culture when it is pretty—enjoying the music, food, culture, and beauty of our people—but remaining silent about our oppression and refusing to see how the beauty of our culture was largely born out of necessity. It hurts students when their teachers acknowledge only what black people have done *for* this country and not what this country has done *to* them.

But how encouraging is it to know that we stand in a powerful political position where we can directly influence and break this silence?

Begin by confronting your own biases—about yourself, your students, your fellow educators, the world. This process is essential; if educators don't do this, think about how much damage we could do to the open, vulnerable minds of our students. In particular, examine your feelings about the police. And, regardless of your personal feelings about law enforcement, it is critical to understand that many black and brown students have incredibly negative perceptions about the police. This difficult understanding on the part of teachers can hopefully lead to dialogue and healing in schools.

Once you've done the inner work of evaluating your own comfort levels and examining your biases, start the conversation. You might begin by admitting to students that—like them—you are scared, frustrated, angry, confused, hurt, or uncomfortable. Students at any age, especially black and brown students, understand these feelings and will appreciate your humility, compassion, and vulnerability. This is how you lay the foundation.

Next, you might begin to explain why you are feeling this way, although many students will already know why. And then, after you've set the stage for conversation, step back, sit down, and be quiet. Let your students lead. Let them speak and ask questions. Allow them, for once, the opportunity to be "in front" of what they are feeling rather than reacting to it.

I like to incorporate the practice of a silent dialogue. To engage students around the police killings of black youth and adults in recent years, I opened with a general question and then placed large chart paper on the floor on which I wrote other questions and asked students to respond silently (with the exception of clarifying the questions or making sure that students were up-to-date on current events). I allowed students to express themselves freely and respond to each other on the paper. This is a tactic that may be helpful if you are truly uncomfortable with this topic and don't know where to begin.

Some students wanted to discuss aloud so we did. I jumped in only to guide or challenge statements that were not aiding the dialogue in a positive way, but I did this in a way that affirmed the students.

This is a beautiful practice. Students come into the classroom with ideas, hearts, passions, mindsets, and understandings about their own humanity. They have been students of the news and their families' stories and experiences without you; they don't necessarily need you in order to understand certain aspects of the world. So if you feel that the conversation is too heavy or that the weight of having to end racism is in your lesson plan, humble yourself and relax. It isn't. Your students need you to allow them space, not to fix the world.

Literature teachers like myself have all the tools necessary to break the silence. Literature is about discussion, awareness, and critical thinking. Writers throughout history have used their pens and pencils to challenge the very structures that still harm our students today. They have done the work for us. Choose a revolutionary book and *really* teach it. Create units around James Baldwin, Richard Wright, Toni Morrison, Alice Walker, Michelle Alexander, and Ta-Nehisi Coates, who, like Baldwin, forewarns all black sons of the dark hours that might soon overtake them.

History teachers, teach your students about what *actually* propelled and sustained the civil rights movement—how the boycotts hit white people in their pocketbooks and how black activists used the media to show the world the brutality of white supremacist police officers—as opposed to a simplified and erroneous account of a docile Rosa Parks who was simply too tired to give up her seat. Remind students that the outrage and outcry of Trayvon Martin's and Alton Sterling's families echo the cries of Emmett Till's mother whose screams exceeded grief, all of them revealing an acknowledgment that their loved ones had become martyrs.

Science teachers, have students research how science was used to justify the myths that promoted black inferiority. This could be followed by a unit on the black scientists whose contributions have greatly advanced their fields. Include information about the Tuskegee experiments and facts about Henrietta Lacks's death so that students understand that black bodies have too often been used, manipulated, and destroyed.

Be on guard against false narratives about how all white people are bad or racists and all African Americans are saints or martyrs. We also cannot remain silent about incidents like the attacks on police in Dallas and Baton Rouge. Teach about the white people who marched with Dr. King and lift their voices in the Black Lives Matter movement today. Teach about white parents who cry out over the lives of slain black children as they would grieve for their own. This is essential if we are to allow our children, and our world, to heal. Teaching as an act of resistance and teaching as an act of healing are not mutually exclusive.

Finally, learn from and for your students. Hear their needs, listen to their struggles—and don't shy away just because you may not understand them. Immerse yourself in literature that matters and that sharpens your zeal for human rights, social justice, and teaching. Connect yourself with others who are doing this work.

And when you don't have the words and can't plan the lessons, don't just say nothing; say exactly what you are feeling. That will mean more to your students than you may ever know.

Black Teachers, Black Youth, and Reality Pedagogy

Christopher Emdin

*Christopher Emdin is an associate professor in the Department of Mathematics,
Science, and Technology at Teachers College, Columbia University, where
he also serves as director of the Science Education Program and associate
director of the Institute for Urban and Minority Education. He is the creator
of the #HipHopEd social media movement and the author of* For White
Folks Who Teach in the Hood . . . and the Rest of Y'all Too.

YOUNG BLACK BROTHERS MOVE WITH AN ELEGANT STRUT THAT IS HALF walk and half dance. Sisters move with noble grace that is half class and half sass. Many Black teachers who teach in Black schools do so for the opportunity to witness these moments. The decision to teach is often more mystical and intuitive than practical. Black teachers teach to create moments of magic and freedom.

In an era where test scores and behavior management have become the chief markers of successful teaching of Black youth, Black teachers have been forced to adopt inhumane pedagogies and develop the concomitant personas that are necessary for their implementation. Unfortunately, the nature of teaching and learning today sees little value in what actually draws Black teachers to teach. And there is little space for Black teachers to explore their emotional connections to youth, a tragedy often exacerbated by an imposed pedagogy that stifles opportunities for authentic relationships with young people.

While reports and research consistently document the achievement gap between Black students and their counterparts from other racial backgrounds, few acknowledge the structures and practices that contribute to that gap. There is no consistent attention to how Black teachers (particularly Black males) are pushed into becoming managers of behavior whose roles in schools are closer to being wardens than teachers.[1] Furthermore, there is little to no recognition of the ways that the entire schooling enterprise becomes one that celebrates Whiteness, or closeness to it, for both teachers and students.

All too often, Black bodies are only welcome in White institutions if they hold White supremacist perspectives of Black youth. Many educators have heard their students use the label "Oreo," a term that grew out of young people's search for language to describe Black people who in some way—or in several ways—are embodying what they know to be White cultural norms. What does it mean when being an "Oreo"—Black on the outside and White on the inside (or in your thinking and practice)—has become a requirement for teaching Black children?

More than ever schools where Black children come to be educated must be willing to accept that there are ways of looking at the world, modes of communication, and approaches to teaching and learning that are unique to Black people. While Blackness is not monolithic, celebrations of the varied forms of Blackness for teachers and students are essential for effective teaching. When White, middle-class norms or ideals are the benchmark for success, Black children fail and we fail Black children.

Schools can equip educators with tools to support the intangible spiritual dimensions of Black teachers teaching Black students. In particular, a pedagogy of healing for both the teacher and the student can begin. This type of pedagogy requires a space for dialogue about the social and psychological baggage that comes from being Black in White schools. White schools are not defined by the constitution of the student population. They are schools where White, middle-class norms have been used as the template for teacher effectiveness and student learning. A pedagogy that unravels and challenges this dynamic requires dialogue about the public image of Blackness and its relationship to the myth that Black students and families lack the desire or ability to be academically successful.

Black teachers endure a constant preoccupation with who they should be when they're teaching that diminishes their availability to fully engage in the type of teaching and learning that is birthed from seeing the beauty of the Blackness of students. They face a conundrum that positions ways to teach that are often intuitive against teaching scripts they are given that require performing a "teacher role" that undermines who they are. Black students respond to this confusion by shutting down to teachers, who could otherwise serve as amazing role models and essential motivators.

The Seven C's of Reality Pedagogy

Reality pedagogy is an approach to teaching that responds to the realities of the students' and teacher's experiences, and constructs a framework for teaching that responds to it. For Black teachers teaching Black students, the tools of reality pedagogy function to restore what is intuitive about Black teaching and learning. These tools reignite a passion for teaching that Black teachers are robbed of in traditional schools. They also provide Black students with opportunities for agency that they are traditionally denied because of misperceptions/misrepresentations of the ways they naturally engage and the attachment of these natural inclinations to anti-school identities.

The tools for reality pedagogy are: co-generative dialogues, co-teaching, cosmopolitanism, context, content, competition, and curation. Enacting these tools helps youth to think critically, make keen observations, support these observations with facts, and engage in dialogue. Most importantly, these tools give Black teachers (and others) an opportunity to get feedback from Black students about how they are experiencing teaching. They move Black teachers and their students to develop connections to each other that reveal their shared humanity. These tools call forth the communality that is inherent in Blackness. The tools also function to strip away the conditioned responses of Black teachers to the flawed structures of schooling, revealing their true academic selves.

Co-generative Dialogues

In co-generative dialogues, four to six students and their teacher—during lunch, before or after school—engage in a conversation about the classroom. These dialogues provide an opportunity for teachers to have discussions with students about the classroom in the absence of formal classroom structures that encourage Black students to act disinterested in learning. These dialogues allow the teacher to have conversations with Black students about how the teacher can better meet their specific academic needs, and they create spaces for students to present their true selves to the teacher.

To create the conditions for these dialogues, the teacher:

- Selects students to participate based on different types of academic roles—e.g., high-achieving and low-achieving students.
- Tells students that participating in the dialogues is voluntary and that the teacher's goal is to become a more effective teacher.
- Ensures that all participants in the dialogues have equal turns to talk by soliciting responses from all students.
- Ensures that all talk is respectful of other participants. The teacher also asks all participants to listen attentively and allow their peers to complete their thoughts before responding. The phrase "one mic" is repeated when this rule is violated by any member of the group, so students can manage each other and maintain a fruitful dialogue.

The conversation must generate an action plan for addressing an issue raised in dialogue.

Co-teaching

In traditional co-teaching, a novice teacher observes or assists an expert teacher. In reality pedagogy with Black students, co-teaching positions the student as the expert and allows him to teach the class. Allowing the student to be the teacher moves beyond traditional co-teaching and empowers the Black student by allowing him/her to become engaged in class and validated for enacting a positive and more academic behavior.

Co-teaching in reality pedagogy can be supported through the following steps:

Before class, the teacher:
- Invites Black students who have been engaged in cogenerative dialogues to be the initial co-teachers.
- Assigns these student-teachers to design a lesson.
- Does a quick review of the lesson plan before class to ensure that content is reflected accurately.

During class, the teacher:
- Sits in the seat of the student-teacher and in the view of the student-teacher.
- Takes notes on the student's teaching, focusing on modes of interaction, use of analogy/metaphor, and other types of phrases used to support learners who are struggling with content.
- Pays close attention to parts of the lesson where the content delivered may not be correct and guides the instruction (by raising a hand as a traditional student would) only when there are issues with the content.

After class, the teacher:
- Engages in a co-generative dialogue with the student so he can reflect on the lesson taught, and the teacher can ask questions about the nuances of the lesson based on his notes.
- Teaches the same lesson students previously taught to another class using techniques from the student's lesson.
- Discusses with the student-teacher the content delivered during the class and how the Black student who co-teaches can help other students who are still struggling to understand the subject.

Cosmopolitanism

A philosophy of cosmopolitanism holds that all human beings feel an inherent need to be responsible for each other in some way. Developing a cosmopolitan ethos in the classroom is a responsibility that teachers of Black students should take seriously. Students must feel that they have roles in the classroom that allow them to be responsible for each other and that allow others to recognize that they have value in the classroom. Once this takes root, Black youths become connected to the physical structure of the classroom and then can become connected to academics. For example, students may be asked to be in charge of collecting homework in the classroom or handing out laptops or other materials. When these roles are enacted consistently, and youth begin to see that they are needed in the classroom, they are more apt to express their true interests in performing well academically.

To create a cosmopolitan classroom, the teacher:
- Identifies the roles and responsibilities for tasks that make the class run smoothly.
- Invites Black students to select roles they want to take on.
- Dedicates the first weeks of school to explicitly discussing the roles of students.
- Changes roles at significant points in the school year—school breaks, semesters, etc.—and transitions youths from roles related to organizing the classroom to roles that support academic success.

Context

Teachers and students bringing symbolic artifacts that are of significance to Black students into the classroom is a powerful way to create learning spaces that value Black life. Artifacts are objects in the students' lives that connect to the in-class lesson. For example, rap songs, pictures from the streets students come from, and other objects that directly relate to what's usually associated with negative attributes of Black students should be used to connect to them academically.

For teachers, finding artifacts from the contexts where youth are embedded will require them to go where Black students spend the most time. There must be a willingness to visit their neighborhoods, watch the television programs that they watch, and listen to music that they like. This approach connects the teacher to the learner in complex ways that only become revealed when students start making connections to these artifacts on their own. Furthermore, it allows the teacher to display the effort involved in making the subject relevant to Black students. For example, youths can be encouraged to create rap songs about the content, pictures from local parks can be used to explain science concepts, and pop culture magazines can be used as the text for English lessons.

Content

Content is not only about the academic work the teacher is responsible for covering; it is also about a teacher's willingness to expose and embrace the limitations of his own content knowledge.

In this step, teachers commend Black students for finding inconsistencies in what the teacher is sharing and allow them to share these inconsistencies publicly. The process requires the teacher's willingness to make statements such as "I don't know" and "that's a good question" when Black students pose questions. Demonstrating this humility helps create a classroom environment where vulnerability is welcome. Acknowledging that education isn't about a completed body of knowledge and that the teacher does not have all of the answers expands student perceptions about the nature of learning. When Black students understand that they aren't merely being expected to memorize material from an accepted body of information, they become more willing to embrace this new classroom environment.

Competition

For far too many Black students, their value is seen only on the sports field or court. In these settings, the contexts are created for them to maximize their output. There is space to practice, a locker room that is comfortable, and other resources are provided to allow them to compete on the highest level. However, when it comes to academic competition, Black students are put in positions where their comfort around how they express themselves or showcase their talent is not allowed to flourish. Competition in reality pedagogy relates to the ways that Black students are allowed to academically compete with each other using forms of cultural expression that are aligned with their out-of-school lives. When the methods for expressing academic content make Black youth comfortable, competing with their peers around this task or activity sharpens and enhances their academic skill. Take for example the Science Genius competition where youth across a number of urban cities engage in rap competitions around science content. For these youth, rap is a comfortable mode of sharing information. Creating a competition that connects to academic content using this tool has yielded great results in science content knowledge acquisition.

Curation

Curation is the last step of reality pedagogy and involves a deliberate collecting and reflecting on artifacts related to teaching and learning by young people for the purpose of helping their teachers to create better classroom experiences that reflect the needs of the students. With curation in reality pedagogy, this process is also engaged in by teachers and includes video recordings of shared experiences, community events, and other significant moments that reflect the realities of those capturing the experiences. Once the events and artifacts have been captured, students and their teacher group them by theme and relation to aspects of the classroom, and then use them as a tool for the teacher's professional development. With Black teachers and their students, connections across artifacts that they decide to curate reveal shared understandings aligned to the Black experience that may have been obscured by curriculum and other school structures. The process of collecting, grouping, and discussing what has been gathered together becomes the seedbed for ongoing connections and provides the teacher with tools that can be used in instruction. Most importantly, the artifacts that have been curated serve as items that can be used for upcoming co-generative dialogues, and the steps of reality pedagogy can then repeat while fostering strong connections between the Black teacher and students.

Conclusion

Given the immense social, scientific, and economic challenges facing young people today and tomorrow, ending the persistence of achievement gaps is essential. Educators must be willing to move beyond political correctness, stop rehashing approaches that have not worked for decades, and stop paying lip service to meeting the needs of Black students without changing their practices. Acknowledging the differences between Black students and their counterparts and building on students' unique strengths by enacting reality pedagogy is a first step.

Notes

1. Christopher Emdin, "Why Black Men Quit Teaching," *New York Times*, August 27, 2016.

How One Elementary School Sparked a Citywide Movement to Make Black Students' Lives Matter

Wayne Au and Jesse Hagopian

Wayne Au is a professor in the School of Educational Studies at the University of Washington Bothell and an editor for Rethinking Schools. *A proud product of Seattle public schools, Dr. Au is an old-school hip-hop head and retired DJ whose work has focused generally on critical education theory, critical policy analysis, and teaching for social justice.*

Jesse Hagopian teaches ethnic studies and is the co-advisor to the Black Student Union at Seattle's Garfield High School—the site of the historic boycott of the MAP test in 2013. He is the editor of the book More Than a Score: The New Uprising Against High-Stakes Testing *and also an editor of* Rethinking Schools.

IT WAS THE MORNING OF SEPTEMBER 16, 2016, AND A CONSCIOUS PARTY of resistance, courage, and community uplift was happening on the sidewalk in front of John Muir Elementary in Seattle. Dozens of Black men were lined up from the street to the school doorway, giving high-fives and praise to all the students who entered as part of a locally organized event called "Black Men Uniting to Change the Narrative." African American drummers pounded defiant rhythms. Students smiled and laughed as they made their way to the entrance. And teachers and parents milled about in #BlackLivesMatter T-shirts, developed and worn in solidarity with the movement to make Black lives matter at John Muir Elementary.

You never would have known that, just hours before, the school was closed and emptied as bomb-sniffing dogs scoured the building looking for explosives.

That September morning was the culmination of a combination of purposeful conversations among John Muir administration and staff, activism, and media attention. John Muir Elementary sits in Seattle's Rainier Valley, and its student population reflects the community: 68 percent of Muir's roughly four hundred students qualify for free or reduced lunch, 33 percent are officially designated transition bilingual, 10 percent are Hispanic, 11 percent are Asian American, 11 percent identify as multiracial, and almost 50 percent are African American—mostly a mix of East African immigrants and families from this historically Black neighborhood.

By that autumn, John Muir Elementary had been actively working on issues of race equity, with special attention to Black students, for months. The previous year, Muir's staff began a deliberate process of examining privilege and the politics of race. With the support of both the school and the PTA, Ruby Bridges—who as a child famously desegregated the all-white William Frantz Elementary School in New Orleans in 1960—had also visited Muir as part of a longer discussion of racism in education among staff and students. During end-of-the-summer professional development, with the support of administration and in the aftermath of the police killings of Alton Sterling and Philando Castile, school staff read and discussed an article on #BlackLivesMatter and renewed their commitment to working for racial justice at Muir.

As part of these efforts, an African American male student-support worker, DeShawn Jackson, organized the "Black Men Uniting to Change the Narrative" event for that September morning, and in solidarity, school staff decided to wear T-shirts that read "Black Lives Matter/We Stand Together/John Muir Elementary," designed by the school's art teacher.

A local TV station reported on the teachers wearing #BlackLives

Matter T-shirts, and as the story went public, political tensions exploded. Soon the white supremacist, hate group–fueled news source Breitbart picked up the story, and the right-wing police-support group Blue Lives Matter publicly denounced the effort. Hateful emails and phone calls began to flood the John Muir administration and the Seattle school board, and then the horrifying happened: Someone made a bomb threat against the school. Even though the threat was deemed not very credible by authorities, out of extreme caution, Seattle Public Schools (SPS) officially canceled the "Black Men Uniting to Change the Narrative" event at Muir.

All of this is what made that September morning all the more powerful. The bomb-sniffing dogs found nothing and school was kept open that day. The drummers drummed and the crowd cheered every child coming through the doors of John Muir Elementary. Everyone was there in celebration, loudly proclaiming that, yes, despite the racist and right-wing attacks, despite the official cancellation, and despite the bomb threat, the community of John Muir Elementary would not be cowed by hate and fear. Black men showed up to change the narrative around education and race. School staff wore their #BlackLivesMatter T-shirts and devoted the day's teaching to issues of racial justice: all bravely and proudly celebrating their power. In the process, this single South Seattle elementary school galvanized a growing citywide movement to make Black lives matter in Seattle schools.

Organizing Across the District

Inspired by that bold action, members of the Social Equality Educators (SEE), a rank-and-file organization of union educators, invited a few John Muir staff to a meeting to offer support and learn more about their efforts. The Muir educators' story explaining how and why they organized for Black lives moved everyone in attendance, and the SEE members began discussing taking the action citywide.

Everyone agreed that there were potential pitfalls of doing a citywide Black students' lives matter event. The John Muir teachers had a race and equity team and dedicated professional development time from the previous year to discuss institutional racism, and they had collectively come to the decision as an entire school to support the action and wear the shirts. What would it mean at a different school if some teachers wore the shirts and taught anti-racist lessons, and others didn't? What if only a few dozen teachers across Seattle wore the shirts—would that send the wrong message? What if other schools received threats? What if those threats materialized?

These and other considerations fueled an important discussion and debate among SEE members, and highlighted the need to educate our communities about why this action was urgently needed. However, with the videos of police killing Philando Castile and Alton Sterling fresh in the minds of SEE members, the group decided that to not publicly declare that Black lives matter would be a message in and of itself.

And it wasn't just the police murder of Black people that motivated SEE to organize action across the school system. It was also because of the institutional racism infecting the Seattle Public Schools. Seattle has an alarming pattern of segregation both between and within schools, with intensely tracked advanced classes overwhelmingly populated with white students. Moreover, the Department of Education's 2013 investigation found that Seattle schools suspended Black students at about four times the rate of white students for the same infractions.[1]

SEE members decided that on October 19, 2016, they would all wear Black Lives Matter shirts to school and voted to create a second T-shirt design that included "#SayHerName." The African American Policy Forum created this hashtag in the wake of Sandra Bland's death while in the custody of Waller County, Texas, police, to raise awareness about police violence against women, to raise awareness about police violence against Black women, and to raise awareness about police violence particularly against Black queer women and Black transgender women.

As part of this action, SEE also developed a three-point policy proposal that would serve as an ongoing campaign to support Black Lives Matter in schools and aid in the struggle against institutional racism:

- Support ethnic studies in all schools.
- Replace zero-tolerance discipline with restorative justice practices.
- De-track classes within the schools to undo the racial segregation that is reinforced by tracking.

In addition, SEE voted to bring a resolution to the Seattle Education Association (SEA), the union representing Seattle's educators, to ask them to publicly declare support for the action by the John Muir teachers and community, and to call on all teachers across the district to actively support the October 19 action.

At the September SEA Representative Assembly, SEE member Sarah Arvey, a white special-education teacher, brought forward the following resolution:

- Whereas the SEA promotes equity and supports anti-racist work in our schools; and,
- Whereas we want to act in solidarity with our members and the community at John Muir who received threats based on their decision to wear Black Lives Matter T-shirts as part of an event with "Black Men United to Change the Narrative"; and,
- Whereas the SEA and SPS promote Race and Equity teams to address institutionalized racism in our schools and offer a space for dialogue among school staff; and,
- Therefore be it resolved that the SEA Representative Assembly endorse and participate in an action wearing Black Lives Matter T-shirts on Wednesday, October 19, 2016, with the intent of showing solidarity, promoting anti-racist practices in our schools, and creating dialogue in our schools and communities.

SEE members expected a difficult debate at the SEA Representative Assembly, and many didn't think the resolution would pass. But they underestimated the impact of the ongoing protests against police brutality and racism that were sweeping school campuses. Inspired by San Francisco 49ers quarterback Colin Kaepernick, the Garfield High School football team captured headlines around the city and nation when every single player and coach took a knee during the national anthem—and maintained that action for the entire season. The protest spread to the girls' volleyball team, the marching band, the cheerleaders, and many other high school sports teams across Seattle. When it came time for the SEA vote, the resolution to support Black Lives Matter at School day passed unanimously.

As word got out about the SEA Representative Assembly vote, and in reaction to the threats against John Muir Elementary earlier in the month, allies also began to step forward in support of making Black Students' Lives Matter. The Seattle NAACP quickly endorsed the event and lent its support. Soup for Teachers, a local parent organizing group formed to support the 2015 SEA strike, and the executive board of the Seattle Council Parent Teacher Student Association (SCPTSA) also endorsed the action and joined in solidarity.

SEE helped gather representatives from these organizations for an October 12 press conference to explain why parents, educators, and racial justice advocates united to declare Black lives matter at school. Predictably, news outlets repeatedly asked teachers if they thought they were politicizing the classroom by wearing BLM shirts to school. NAACP education chair Rita Green responded directly, "We're here to support families. We're here to support students. When Black lives matter, all lives matter."

Sarah Arvey, of SEE, told reporters, "It's important for us to know the history of racial justice and racial injustice in our country and in our world . . . in order for us to address it. When we're silent, we close off dialogue and we close the opportunity to learn and grow from each other." Other teachers pointed out that students were having discussions all the time in the halls, during sports practice, and outside of school about racism, police violence, and the Black Lives Matter movement. A better question to ask, teachers asserted, would be "Is school going to be relevant to the issues that our students are discussing every day?"

In an effort to build greater solidarity for Seattle educators taking part in the Black Lives Matter at School day, one of us—Wayne—organized a national letter for professors to sign on to in an effort to build support for the action. After only a few days, close to 250 professors, many of them well-recognized scholars in educational research locally and nationally, had signed on. Another letter of support was signed by luminaries such as dissident scholar Noam Chomsky, former MSNBC anchor Melissa Harris-Perry, 1968 Olympic bronze medalist and activist John Carlos, Black Lives Matter co-founder Opal Tometi, noted education author Jonathan Kozol, and Pulitzer Prize–winning journalist Jose Antonio Vargas.

As support for Seattle's Black Lives Matter at School action swelled, in a move that surprised many, the Seattle School District's administration, with no formal provocation from activists or the school board, officially endorsed the event. An October 8 memo read:

> During our #CloseTheGaps kick-off week, Seattle Education Association is promoting October 19 as a day of solidarity to bring focus to racial equity and affirming the lives of our students—specifically our students of color.
>
> In support of this focus, members are choosing to wear Black Lives Matter T-shirts, stickers, or other symbols of their commitment to students in a coordinated effort. SEA is leading this effort and working to promote transformational conversations with staff, families, and students on this issue.
>
> We invite you to join us in our commitment to eliminate opportunity gaps and accelerate learning for each and every student.

At that point, we in Seattle felt that we had accomplished something historic, because for perhaps the first time in Seattle's history, the teachers and the teachers' union, the parents and the PTSA, students and the Seattle School District administration had all reached a consensus support for a very politicized action for racial justice in education.

As the October 19 Black Lives Matter at School day approached, orders for the various Black Lives Matter T-shirts soared. John Muir set up a site where T-shirt purchases would directly benefit the school's racial justice work. SEE's online T-shirt site received some two thousand orders for the BLM shirts, with proceeds going to support racial justice campaigns and a portion going to John Muir. Other schools created their own T-shirt designs specific to their schools. The Seattle schools were now poised for unprecedented mass action for racial justice.

Black Lives Matter at School Day

As October 19 arrived, Garfield High School senior Bailey Adams was in disbelief. She told Seattle's KING 5 News, "There was a moment of like, is this really going to happen? Are teachers actually going to wear these shirts? All of my years I've been in school, this has never been talked about. Teachers have never said anything where they're going to back their students of color."

But sure enough, every school across the city had educators come to school wearing the shirts. Hundreds of teachers took advantage of the day to teach lessons and lead discussions about institutional racism. SEE and Soup for Teachers partnered to make a handout called "Teaching and Mentoring for Racial Justice" that suggested BLM resources for both teachers and parents. The SEA also emailed suggested resources to teachers.

Some schools changed their reader boards to declare "Black Lives Matter." Parents at some elementary schools set up tables by the front entrance with books and resources to help other parents talk to their kids about racism. Many schools coordinated plans for teaching about Black lives, including lessons about movements for racial justice and lessons about the way racism impacts the school system today. Several teachers across the district showed the film *Stay Woke* about the origins of the Black Lives Matter movement, and held class discussions afterward. Some educators used the opportunity to discuss intersectional identities and highlighted how Black and queer women had first launched the #BlackLivesMatter hashtag.

Schools such as Chief Sealth International High School and Garfield High School put up Black Lives Matter posters/graffiti walls, which quickly filled up with anti-racist commentary from students and educators. A teacher at Dearborn Park International Elementary built a lesson plan from a photo of Colin Kaepernick kneeling. To capture the power of the day, educators from most of the schools around the district took group photos wearing the BLM shirts and sent them to the union for publication.

During lunchtime, the Garfield faculty, staff, and students rallied on the front steps of the school. In one of the most moving and powerful moments of the day, Black special-education teacher Janet Du Bois decided she finally had to tell everyone a secret she had been quietly suffering with. In front of all the assembled school community and media she revealed that the police had murdered her son several years ago—and this had happened after he had been failed by the education system and pushed out of school. Fighting through tears, Du Bois said, "When our kids are failed, they have to go to alternative places and end up with their lives hanging in the balance because someone does not care."[2]

To cap off the extraordinary and powerful day, SEE organized a community celebration, forum, and talent showcase that evening that drew hundreds of people. The event was emceed by educator, organizer, poet, attorney, and soon-to-be Seattle mayoral candidate Nikkita Oliver. Spoken word poets, musicians, and the Northwest Tap Connection (made up of predominantly Black youth performers) delighted and inspired the audience. Black youth activists from middle schools and high schools engaged in an onstage discussion about their experience of racism in school and what changes they wanted to see to make the education system truly value their lives. Seahawks Pro Bowl defensive end Michael Bennett came to the event and pledged his support of the movement, saying, "Some people believe the change has to come from the government, but I believe it has to be organic and come from the bottom."

By the end of the day, thousands of educators had reached tens of thousands of Seattle students and parents with a message of support for Black students and opposition to anti-Black racism—with local and national media projecting the message much further. While the educators who launched this movement were quite aware that the institutions of racism remained intact, they also knew those same institutions had been shaken.

Lessons Learned

In many ways we had a successful campaign around making Black lives matter in Seattle schools, and from an organizing perspective, we learned several important lessons. To begin, we learned that one school can make a big difference: a single elementary school bravely took a stand that provided a spark for an already simmering citywide movement and influenced national discussions, as educators in Philadelphia, Rochester, New York, and elsewhere followed suit with similar educationally based #BlackLivesMatter actions.

We also learned that acting in the context of a broader social movement was critical. The police killings of Philando Castile and Alton Sterling in the summer of 2016, as part of the long-standing pattern of Black deaths at the hands of police, ensured that there were ongoing protests and conversations associated with #BlackLivesMatter. This broader movement created the political space and helped garner support for the actions of both John Muir Elementary specifically, and Seattle Public Schools more generally.

In addition, we learned that sometimes when the white supremacists, "alt-right," and right-wing conservatives attack, it can make our organizing stronger and more powerful. In the case of Seattle, it was the avalanche of hateful emails and calls, the right-wing media stories, and the bomb threat against John Muir Elementary that ultimately galvanized teachers and parents across the city.

We also learned that developing a broad base of support was essential to the success of the campaign to make Black student lives matter in Seattle schools. Garnering the official support of the teachers union, the executive board of the Seattle Council PTSA, and even the Seattle Public Schools, as well as inspiring acts of solidarity from scholars and others nationally, helped build a protective web of political support to shield Seattle educators as they moved forward with their action.

In the end, we also learned that with more time and resources we could have done better organizing. For instance, we had to grapple with the fact that when the John Muir Elementary staff made the decision to wear their #BlackLivesMatter T-shirts, it was after they'd participated in sustained discussion and professional development that took place over multiple years. Ideally, all schools would have had the opportunity for similar discussions as part of their typical professional development, so that when a moment like this happened, all school staff would have a stronger basic understanding of racial justice to guide their decision-making.

Another possible improvement would have been to offer a clearer vision of curriculum across the district for the Black Lives Matter at School day. Despite the strength of the "Teaching and Mentoring for Racial Justice" resource handout developed by SEE and Soup for Teachers, the quality and depth of what children at different schools learned on the day of the district-wide event varied wildly from school to school. With just a little more time and resources, we could have provided teachers with a cluster of grade-level-appropriate teaching activities that they could have used on that day if they wanted. In particular this is something that might have helped teachers around the district who wanted to support the action but struggled with ways to explicitly make Black lives matter in their own classroom curriculum.

It wasn't until the end of the school year that we learned two more lessons. The first was that, despite widespread community support for Black Lives Matter at School day, the passive-aggressive racism of some of Seattle's notoriously liberal, white parents had been lurking all along. In a June 2017 story, local news radio station KUOW reported on a series of emails from white parents who live in the more affluent north end of Seattle. According to the story, white parents complained not just about the perceived militancy and politics of the Black Lives Matter in School day in Seattle, but that children couldn't handle talking about racism, and that we should be colorblind because "all lives matter." Importantly, many of these parents openly questioned the existence of racial inequality in Seattle's schools.

The second lesson we learned well after the Black Lives Matter in School day was that our action helped strengthen the political groundwork for a continued focus on racial justice in Seattle Public Schools. On July 5, 2017, the Seattle school board unanimously passed a resolution in support of ethnic studies in Seattle schools in response to a yearlong campaign by the NAACP, SEE, and other social justice groups, including formal endorsement from the Seattle Education Association. While this policy shift happened on the strength of the community organizing for ethnic studies specifically, Seattle's movement to make Black Lives Matter in School demonstrated to the district that there was significant public support for racial justice initiatives in Seattle schools, effectively increasing the official space for other initiatives like ethnic studies to take hold.

Putting the Shirts Back On

The school year ended with a horrific reminder of why we must continue to declare the value of Black lives when on Sunday, June 18, 2017, Seattle police shot and killed Charleena Lyles, a pregnant mother of four, in her own apartment after she called them in fear her home was being burglarized. She was shot down in a hail of bullets in front of three of her kids, two of whom attended public elementary schools in Seattle. The immediate media narrative of her death dehumanized her by focusing on the fact that the police alleged Charleena was wielding a kitchen knife, that she had a history of mental illness and a criminal background. This had become a familiar strategy: the police kill a Black person and then assassinate their character in an attempt to turn public opinion in support of the police.

But in Seattle, there were the countervailing forces of Charleena's organized family, community activists, and Seattle educators who forced a different public discussion about the value of Black lives and the callous disregard of them by unaccountable police. SEE and the SEA immediately put out a call for teachers to put their Black Lives Matter shirts back on—many of which also featured #SayHerName—for a school district–wide action in solidarity with Charleena and her family on June 20. Within three days of Charleena's death, hundreds of teachers came to school wearing heartbreak, rage, and solidarity in the form of their Black Lives Matter T-shirts—with profits from shirt sales this time going to Charleena's family.

That day, a couple hundred educators swelled the ranks of the after-school rally with Charleena's family and hundreds of other supporters at the apartment complex where she had been killed. With educators from her son's schools and all across the district rallying to Charleena's side, the press was compelled to run stories talking about her as a woman, as a parent of Seattle schoolchildren, and as a person with talents and struggles like everyone else.

Seattle's Black Lives Matter at School day is only a beginning. Having nearly three thousand teachers wear T-shirts to school one day doesn't magically end anti-Black racism or white supremacy. If that were the case, then perhaps Charleena Lyles would still be alive today to drop her kids off at school, chat with other parents on the playground, and watch the children play.

But something powerful and important did happen in Seattle. At John Muir Elementary, the school staff and community stood strong against white supremacist hate, and across Seattle Public Schools, teachers and parents found a way to stand in solidarity with Black students and their families. In the process, the public dialogue about institutionalized racism in Seattle schools was pushed forward in concrete ways. And while we have so much more work to do, in the end, what happened in Seattle showed that educators have an important role to play in the movement for Black lives. When they rise up across the country to join this movement—both inside the school and outside on the streets—institutions of racism can be challenged in the search for solidarity, healing, and justice.

Notes

1. Keith Ervin and Maureen O'Hagan, "Feds Probing Seattle Schools' Treatment of Black Students," *Seattle Times*, March 5, 2013.

2. "2,000 Seattle Teachers Wear Black Lives Matter Shirts to School," K5News, October 19, 2016, https://www.king5.com/article/news/local/seattle/2000-seattle-teachers-wear-black-lives-matter-shirts-to-school/281-338419052.

The Fire

Sarah Ishmael and Jonathan Tunstall in conversation

Sarah Ishmael, a former elementary school teacher in Baton Rouge, Louisiana, is a doctoral candidate at the University of Wisconsin-Madison where she researches differing conceptualizations of humanity and how they relate to curriculum, students, and teachers. She co-authored "Stagger Lee: Millennial Teachers' Perspectives, Politics and Prose" in Mary Dilworth's Millennial Teachers of Color *and authored "Dysconcious Racism, Class Privilege and TFA" in T. Jameson Brewer and Kathleen deMarrais's edited volume* Teach for America Counter-Narratives.

Jonathan Tunstall taught middle-school social studies for eight years in Harlem, New York, and is pursuing a PhD at the University of Wisconsin-Madison. He is a hip-hop and teaching artist who is currently working with the Whoopensocker education residency to get elementary students excited about writing through creating short stories and plays.

It's gonna rain
It's gonna rain
You better get ready and bear this in mind
God showed Noah, the rainbow sign
He said it won't be water but fire next time.
Way back in the bible days,
Noah told the people it's gonna rain
but when he told them they paid him no
mind and when it happen they were left

behind, I tell you
It's gonna rain
It's gonna rain
You better get ready and bear this in mind
God showed Noah, the rainbow sign
He said it won't be water but fire next time.

ELDER JAMES BALDWIN PENNED A LETTER TO HIS NEPHEW, BETTER known as the book *The Fire Next Time*, that ends with the Negro spiritual, "It's Gonna Rain," above. In his letter, Baldwin does not refer often to fires, but near the middle, he writes about at least two different kinds of fires. He discusses the fire God promises Noah; the red-hot flames of such cosmic vengeance for the cruelty he saw in humankind. And he talks about fire as a personal experience of human cruelty from which all black people must "snatch our [personhood], our identities."[1] He notes that even if we do not survive the fire, we gain something and learn something about human life itself that no school or church on earth can teach. We achieve our own unshakable authority.

"In order to save our lives, we are forced to look beneath appearances, to take nothing for granted and to read the meanings behind words." This has been the experience of generations of Negroes, he continues, "and it helps to explain how [we] have endured and how [we] have been able to produce children of kindergarten age who can walk through mobs to get to school. [What we do] . . . demands great spiritual resilience not to hate; not to teach your children to hate."

As black educators, we confront fires every day in our communities: Trayvon Martin, Tamir Rice, Cameron Tillman, Laquan McDonald, Vonderrit Myers Jr., Micheal Brown, Rekia Boyd, the Charleston church massacre, Philando Castile. And there are the fires *in our schools*, such as a cop flipping over the desk of a young woman in Columbia, South Carolina, in an attempt to take her out of the classroom.[2] We breathe this fire. It's not just the fire next time, it's the fire we live in now.

The Fire Next Time gives a sharp, sober, beautiful hope, a clarity and confidence that validates the realness of the experiences of black woman educators. It also provides a language to describe the invisible forces I, Sarah, felt burning my skin and insides when I taught black and brown students in Baton Rouge. Teaching within the trauma of local and national violence against black children within school institutions that promote that very violence feels like being engulfed in an invisible blue fire 24/7. Elder Baldwin's words pour onto my soul like calming, clean rainwater.

I, Jon, taught in Harlem for eight years. More than Baldwin's words, Emily Raboteau's chapter in *The Fire This Time* extinguishes that fire—temporarily—for me.[3] Reading her essay transported me back to the Harlem. I lived on 135th and 5th, a few short blocks away from a mural she admires. I passed that mural every day. I remember feeling mesmerized the first time that I saw it: a voice of resistance, a civics lesson, a dope piece of art. The mural accomplished what I toiled for daily as an educator: arming students with knowledge, instilling them with pride, and affirming their culture while doing it. Raboteau describes the mural as armor. This armor surrounded me as I entered into the classroom every day, ready for war. Not war with the students I taught, but with messages of racial inferiority seeping into their consciousness. These messages were reinforced every time they saw someone who looked like them killed with impunity, and every time they took stock of the condition of Harlem, situated right next to Columbia University's Morningside Heights.

We—a black, cis-male teacher from L.A. and a black, cis-female military brat from everywhere and nowhere—have both taught in the fire that scorches our throats and the psyches of our students. We see in Baldwin's letter to his nephew a warning, a wondering, and a charge.

The warning is about what will happen to humankind if we fail to raise our own consciousness of each other's lived experiences and to create empathy with one another so that all of us can survive. Baldwin ponders the fate of the people he knows and loves, the comrades from his youth, his "buddies in those wine- and urine-stained hallways" and wonders, "What will happen to all that beauty?"[4]

And the charge:

Everything now, we must assume, is in our hands; we have no right to assume otherwise. If we—and now I mean the relatively conscious whites and the relatively conscious blacks, who must, like lovers, insist on, or create, the consciousness of others—do not falter in our duty now, we may be able, handful that we are, to end the racial nightmare, and achieve our country, and change the history of the world. If we do not dare everything, the fulfillment of that prophecy, re-created from the Bible in song by the slave, is upon us: God gave Noah the rainbow sign, No more water, the fire next time!

His charge is to insist on or create the consciousness of others to end the racial nightmare and change the history of the world. As teachers, what *do* we do to fulfill his charge? What do we do to change the hearts of men through raising our own and others' consciousness? What do we do to deal with both the fire now, and the fire coming *next time*?

Sarah: You taught in Harlem for eight years before coming to grad school, yea?

Jon: Mm-hmmm—eight years, that's right.

Sarah: What lessons do you teach, projects do you assign, what sources of inspiration that inspire your teaching and projects to raise consciousness? As a black teacher in Harlem?

Jon: What did *you* teach and do to raise consciousness as a black teacher in the South?

Sarah: Hah! I didn't teach as long as you did, but one thing I learned to do was to *listen.*

When we are with students, with parents, even with ourselves, we have to listen on different levels.

Jon: One thing I try to do is to keep up the tradition that black scholars and artists have of flippin' something out of nothin.' Change the knowledge . . .

Sarah: Yes, so it reflects us, black people—from the diaspora or from wherever we are placed—as *actual* sources of knowledge that the world needs to learn from.

Jon: Yea yea yea! That's that #hiphoped![5] I went into teaching to teach authentic history. The way it's taught makes us feel like the white man is the pinnacle of evolution, i.e., the pioneer spirit, the legend of the frontiersman, and then a sanitized version of Dr. King, or Reconstruction portrayed through white supremacy.

The classroom felt like a battlefield at times. Trial by fire is what most veteran teachers called it the first few years. Social justice teachers are forced to negotiate space for teaching an anti-racist curriculum. It seems like common sense. Empowering the students, exposing racism, and giving them tools to navigate America's racist system. However, this curriculum is not Regents' board approved. This curriculum must be fought for and placed in conjunction with traditional lessons that teach rote memorization of facts and the five-paragraph essay. However, the New York City Department of Education–issued Houghton Mifflin textbook did nothing to defend my students from the psychic attacks society assaulted them with daily, inundating them with ideas of inferiority. My rage was channeled into my lessons. Before I ever stepped into the classroom, I had already decided that I was willing to get fired. I had already decided that my contribution to the fight against racial oppression would take place in the classroom.

Sarah: Legit. That's why I am in graduate school now—to help make the curriculum our students *need* instead of learning from a curriculum that erases who they are and the idea that we have knowledge in ourselves as black people that others need to hear. When I was teaching, my students only wanted one thing from me: to teach them well. I was an elementary school teacher and then I moved to a middle-school special-education team. It was *very* hard to find curriculum that showed them that they themselves could create knowledge, that we as black people are a *source* of knowledge.

Will Garcia, a PhD student at the University of Kansas, posts these articles that our students in middle schools and *elementary* schools need to know like, "Today in 1879, the Zulu defeated the British at Isandlwana Mountain" by Thandiwe Matyobeni,[6] and "Let's stop erasing the history of Caribbean indentured labour" by Vanesha Singh.[7] Our histories are just now being reclaimed from Eurocentric curriculum. I didn't have access to people writing authentic histories about black (in my case Afro-Caribbean) people back then. *That's* what my students wanted to know. That's what they were curious about. Not the backwards-planned lessons created from statewide tests. My fifth graders (at the time) knew an insult to their intelligence when they saw one. And anything less than curriculum that also reflected their lived experiences was exactly that.

Jon: The first one was the article, I was a part of an organization called Facing History and Ourselves.[8] They have great articles. But still, all that's made for high school students. When I taught, I had to rearrange some things, chunk ideas in the article together. For example, I taught a unit on race. I played a clip from the documentary *Race: The Power of an Illusion* and discussed the idea of race as scientific nonsense with my students.[9] We talked about race in the Latina/o American community and the complications of it. Like, what was Ayesha's issue with Telemundo? She hates the portrayal of white Latino/a Americans on that channel. We discussed why. Then I gave them readings on the construction of race, that I modified. It's really hard to find critical things written on race that aren't college level. The questions that I asked them were: (1) Is black history still necessary? (2) Is hip-hop music harmful/helpful? (3) Are Dominicans black? (4) Should we live in a colorblind society? I had a bunch of topics in a hat. I gave them five to ten minutes to come up with a brief, then I let them have a small group discussion based on their notes. It was a fishbowl and the other students took notes on their conversation.

They were into it after the clip. The most controversial question for them was whether or not Dominicans were black. Some students were adamant that they were black, the majority were not. They can handle these "controversial" issues.

Sarah: OF COURSE they can. What do people think they are doing on social media all day? They are creating and defending their identities and their personhood using labels and words that are attached to long-destructive histories. They make and remake themselves as middle schoolers with these "controversial issues" because they LIVE those "controversial issues" all day every day. It's not just some "adolescent drama" that we can roll our eyes about. There are real questions about life, history, identity, personhood, and economy that drive their posts and their online presence.

Jon: This lesson was the first time my students ever had a structured conversation about race versus ethnicity. Participation was dope. You know getting a discussion going in middle school is difficult. They responded to specific questions, they posed questions to each other. A lot of students were talkin' all over each other and more importantly *to* each other. It was great.

Sarah: Right? Students *do* this critical work all the time. We need to be able to make curriculum do what Elder James and Emily Raboteau do for you and me. I mean ultimately what you were doing at the time was helping them mediate their lived experience with historical information that helped them see the rules that not only govern their perceptions of themselves, but also the perceptions of others. I tried to teach so that what my students would know that the way things are now—even down to the math concepts I taught—have been created by people, and not just white people. Knowledge isn't simply "natural," like ultimate knowledge.

I hope I taught them to go about actively deciphering knowledge, so that they can see themselves as whole persons who can change knowledge itself rather than just sit at a desk and try to memorize a curriculum that teaches us that we are nothing.

Jon: Racism is based on a flawed conceptualization of race as a biological, inherent identity, when in fact it is a social construction whose meaning changes over time, history, and location.

I had my students interpret that definition with me out loud in the class. I think it was important to ask college-level questions, because they could handle them. I taught them to "code switch" the question by having them rewrite the question in a way that made sense to them. It's important to let them know that how they think and speak are legitimate ways of knowing, processing, and expressing. I had them analyze this quote and relate it to race relations in modern America and in their own personal experience.

When I first gave them the definition they all freaked out, so we rewrote this statement as a class. We came up with "Race is fake and society made it up for different reasons." Then they broke out into small group discussions.

After the end of the forty-minute session, they were into it: *70 percent turned in their homework*, which was truly remarkable. (Less than 40 percent of students in my school typically did their homework.) They loved it. It was a big idea to break down, but people were into the conversations. I had students who . . . it was like pulling teeth to get them to talk, but they were excited to discuss these questions. They had these personal opinions and they were very excited to share them in an academic space as legitimately recognized information and knowledge.

By the end of the unit I had them write an essay and create a video documentary discussing identity. Some interviewed people. You could be completely creative, as long as you addressed (a) what role do you think colorism plays in your life? And (b) how would you describe your identity? Some of them went with culture, some of them went with race, some of them identified with a job.

I had a student who really got into the discussion and was excited to share his opinion in an academic venue. He actually *came* to class. He came to my class because he was a rapper and I was a rapper and we used to spit sometimes. For this particular moment, he saw his information become knowledge worth sharing in an academic setting. He talked about police brutality, accountability, he did the documentary by making a four- to six-minute PowerPoint including his opinion about skin color. He was in the position of an expert in this situation. He was an expert on being a young black man. He lived it, was *in* it, and his expertise was valuable. That's not traditionally recognized because of the slang and because he doesn't speak in a specific academic vernacular.

Sarah: That's powerful.

Jon: It didn't always work all the time! Some of my lessons bombed, but those were some of the things I did in my classroom that helped me deal with "being on fire" all the time. I think these were moves towards answering Elder James's call to insist on and create the consciousness of others—doing my part to end the racial nightmare.

Sarah: Well damn. I think what I like about the activities, prompts, and resources you used are that they start off from the understanding that human consciousness and identity are distorted by hegemonic structures of knowledge. We know curriculum sorts people into persons and nonpersons and that our students *feel* that—like my fifth graders. I think to deal with the fire we teach in now is to be curious, actually ask questions. What are the comparisons between the way the students in critical pedagogy classrooms construct and use knowledge and the way other students who are not in critical pedagogy classrooms construct and use knowledge? What are the differences in the messages they internalize about themselves as people as a result of these different curriculums? What are the differences in how ideologies of knowledge work on them and through them? I wish I would have asked those questions back then. But I do now.

Do you think that's enough?

Jon: We're a part of the puzzle. It's what keeps me going every day. Elder James's warning, his willing, and his charge.

Sarah: I worry that it isn't. But our students are still in that fire and we have a responsibility to do what we can to provide water—some psychic relief. I was feelin' down about it all one day, the warning, the willing, and the charge. I asked my advisor for advice. You know what she did? Gloria emailed me the best thing I ever heard in my life:[10]

> I am sorry to learn of the struggles you are encountering with the students and the self-doubt you may be experiencing. What I am about to say is not meant to sound unsympathetic, but like I have told the eighteen other Black women whose dissertations I've supervised . . . this is really not about you.
>
> It is all about that young Black girl who is sitting in a middle or high school classroom believing that there is absolutely no future for her because someone keeps whispering or sending her messages that Black girls and women are not smart. Your task is to DO THE WORK!

Jon: AHAH HAAAHH! Word.
Sarah: Right!?

Jon: That's how we have kindergarteners that can walk through angry, violent mobs to get to school.

Sarah: No joke. We *all* in this fire. Baldwin was right though. We gain something and learn something about human life itself that nothing else can teach us.

Jon: We achieve our own unshakable authority.

Sarah: That *unshakable* authority. Our work literally changes history. The warning, the willing, and the charge. We 'bout to save the world!

Jon: HAH! Yeah. It's gonna rain, but there ain't gon' be no "fire next time."

Use your smartphone camera function or a QR code scanning app on the QR code above to link directly to a YouTube video performance of "It's Gonna Rain (No More Water but Fire This Time)."

Notes

1. James Baldwin, *The Fire Next Time* (New York: Vintage Books, 1962/1963).

2. Richard Fausset and Ashley Southall, "Video Shows Officer Flipping Student in South Carolina, Prompting Inquiry," *New York Times*, October 26, 2015.

3. Jesmyn Ward, *The Fire This Time* (New York: Scribner, 2016).

4. James Baldwin, *The Fire Next Time* (New York: First Vintage International Edition, 1993), 99.

5. HipHopEd, hiphoped.com.

6. Thandiwe Matyobeni, "Today in 1879, the Zulu defeated the British at Isandlwana Mountain," Briefly.co.za (January 27, 2019), retrieved from: briefly .co.za/22613-today-1879-zulu-defeated-british-isandlwana-mountain.html?fb clid=IwAR1BRyOZzB61m-q4_wCLLVlJ0bBxj2TJT2iRrd5Gd9C_s4kdB2mE 9I1lRIk#22613.

7. Vanesha Singh, "Let's Stop Erasing the History of Caribbean Indentured

Labour," *gal-dem* (January, 20, 2019), retrieved from: gal-dem.com/lets-stop
-erasing-the-history-of-caribbean-indentured-labour/?fbclid=IwAR1xJMnaYt
Zttx3Nt5J4PBt_RHQTpyEv25W83hPlREvGRPsZkr95aeUR6pA.

8. Facing History, Facing Ourselves: facinghistory.org.

9. *Race: The Power of an Illusion*, official website: pbs.org/race/000_General
/000_00-Home.htm.

10. Gloria refers to Gloria Ladson-Billings, author of the book *The Dream-keepers* and teacher educator on the faculty of the University of Wisconsin–Madison School of Education where she is also assistant vice chancellor of Academic Affairs.

Engaging and Embracing Black Parents

Allyson Criner Brown

Allyson Criner Brown, the associate director of Teaching for Change and a family engagement specialist in Washington, DC, works to provide strategies for effectively engaging parents at schools that serve primarily low-income black students.

I WAS HALFWAY THROUGH MY SECOND WEEK OF TEACHING AT AN ALL-black middle school in St. Louis when I realized I should start reaching out to parents. It was August 2006, still the beginning of the school year, and I had not experienced any major class disruptions yet. However, the more vociferous students in my classes were starting to emerge, as were the smiles and snickers that came from their amused peers.

Family engagement was not part of my teacher training, but my instinct told me that I should make a friendly phone call home to establish rapport with families, so that if I did call about poor behavior it would not be the first time they had heard from me. For the next week or so, I spent my evenings and break time calling the home numbers of my 200-plus seventh and eighth graders to introduce myself to their parents and caregivers. I reached an adult at most numbers, and I recall that the majority of conversations began with tension:

"Hello?"

"Yes, hi! This is Ms. Criner, I'm one of your daughter's teachers at school. I was just calling to introduce myself."

"You're calling from the school? What did she do already? Do I have to come up there?"

"No, no! We're having a great start to the year. I just wanted to reach out and let you know that I may touch base from time to time. And here's my phone number—you can call or text me if you ever have a question or need to chat about her schoolwork."

"Oh!" The tone on the other end of the phone would shift. "Well, hi then. Okay, thank you."

Sure enough, within another week I was calling some of the same families back relaying that their child did not have the best day in my class, and that I was letting them know so that we could work together. And I promised to call again to let them know when their child was doing well.

Over the course of my teaching I kept my word, making sure that every negative phone call I made was balanced with at least one positive phone call. In fact, I became known as the teacher who called their homes "all the time" as my students would say (often with an eye roll), and I embraced it.

"I am going to make three phone calls home today to let some of your parents know how good a job you did today," you could hear in my classes several times a month. "If you want to be one of those phone calls then you'll show me by your work and your behavior!"

Looking back on my time in the front of the classroom, I realize that building relationships with my students' families was one of the high-lights of my teaching experience. But after leaving teaching in order to lead family engagement work in Washington, DC, with compara-ble schools and comparable populations for nearly ten years, and now as the parent of a black child in public school, I have some deeper reflections and lessons learned about what it means to actually en-gage black families in their children's education and the life of their schools.

As the manager of the Tellin' Stories parent organizing project of Washington, DC–based Teaching for Change, I have become a well-versed practitioner in the field of family engagement. Teaching for

Change's family engagement approach is informed by racial equity, popular education, community organizing, and effective practices from the research on family engagement.

With the knowledge I have now (hindsight is always 20/20), I can see the positive aspects of my efforts as a classroom teacher to engage families, but also the well-intentioned shortcomings. My interactions with students' families were more positive than most of their other interactions with the school, but, admittedly, I had weaponized my communications with their families as a classroom management strategy. I turned family engagement into a carrot and a stick, as opposed to a collaborative effort with my students' best interests at heart. My communications with families were mostly one-directional, with the goal of making things in my classroom run more smoothly. This was a desirable outcome for me that had tangible benefits for my students, but my well-meaning efforts fell short of high impact family engagement.

Let me pause to acknowledge that with all that teachers are juggling, especially in the modern political context, even well-meaning family engagement can seem out of reach. The fact that I had over two hundred individual students made communicating with families challenging enough on top of my other responsibilities as a classroom teacher. High-stakes testing loomed over us constantly, as did the challenges that come with teaching in high poverty communities. And aside from my own calls and communications home, I did not see much effort from the school to engage parents outside of the traditional means (Back to School Night and parent-teacher conferences), except when there were serious discipline issues. Looking back, I can pat myself on the back for trying, while also applying a critical lens to my own practices and seeing areas for improvement.

Since my time as a teacher, I have come to appreciate just how key family engagement truly is to student success. This is supported by decades of research that conclude family engagement has a direct impact on student achievement,[1] and that **families of *all* races, cultural backgrounds, education, and income levels can have a positive**

influence on their children's learning.[2] There are noted benefits for educators as well, including reduced feelings of isolation, breaking down race and class hierarchies, and creating mutual respect between home and school.[3] An often-cited study of schools in Chicago found that schools with strong family and community ties are more likely to make significant math and reading gains.[4] When schools meaningfully partner with families, including black families, we see greater student achievement and the school gets better as well.

Yet, I am not convinced that authentically engaging black families has been fully embraced or invested in as a strategy to support black students. Generally, low-income, African American parents are often viewed as being less engaged with their children's academics than are middle- and high-income parents.[5] Researchers have found that parents of color and families of immigrant, low-income, and special needs learners are more likely to develop an adversarial relationship with the school.[6]

So, how should we approach engaging black families? I am a huge fan of researchers Anne Henderson, Karen Mapp, and their collaborators who have written about high impact family engagement.[7] We must build relationships with families in intentional, respectful, and ongoing ways. We must link our family engagement efforts to student learning, so that families are engaged as partners in children's learning and not simply shuffled through obligatory activities. We must approach black families as funds of knowledge and build on their strengths, while addressing differences in their understanding and experiences with school and what their children are learning. We must support families in their advocacy, collaborate with them, and share decision-making power—from the individual student up to schoolwide decisions. Our engagements with black families should be interactive, two-directional, and mindful of this mantra that drives Teaching for Change's family engagement approach: "Too often systems, not people, are responsible for creating and maintaining the disconnect between families and schools, and unfortunately, too often people, not systems, are blamed."[8]

What follows are some engagement strategies that offer avenues for involving parents—in particular, those from low-income families of color—in their children's education.

Ice-Breaking Activities

"I'm not sure what to do!" a shy father says, stroking his beard to mask his nervousness after realizing he is the only one without a partner. Other voices chime in with encouragement and suggestions for him to consider. "Hand to hand," he finally says. Then, "Person to person!" he shouts, rushing to link arms with a teacher nearby as the group scrambles to find new partners.

In my work, I have led ice breakers in meetings between parents and teachers that brought people to their feet and smiles to their faces. I recall fondly how fourth grade parents and teachers giggled with uncertainty as I instructed them to stand up, find a partner, and then touch elbow-to-elbow, foot-to-foot, and hip-to-hip before I called out the cue for everyone to switch partners. They rushed faster than their children knowing that the one person left without a partner would take my spot as the leader. The new "leader" then took turn giving directions.

Within five minutes, parents and teachers had each served as the "leader" and roused full-bellied laughs from the group, connecting beyond their titles as people all playing a new game. After I wrapped up the game and settled the group down, we shared observations about the activity, noting how anyone could act as a leader and how sometimes when people were nervous or unsure what to do, others in the group encouraged them. Parents and teachers also noted how good it felt to laugh together and start the meeting on a warm and positive note, even for those who felt hesitant about participating.

When the fourth grade teachers stepped back to the front of the room to thank the parents and caregivers for coming and share the purpose of the meeting, many people still had smiles on their faces. The ice breaker, though, was only the first of many times parent voices were heard in the meeting. Teachers used the remainder of the time to dialogue with parents, sharing activities for parents to support their kids with the "new math" at home, and listening to parents discuss what their kids say they are learning in school. As they left the classroom with take-home packets and math manipulatives, many parents were still smiling after this new experience they had with their child's teachers.

These kinds of interactions that intentionally build relationships and disrupt the power dynamics between parents and teachers change the way both groups see each other and how they share information, and better equip them to support black students.

Valuing Parent Perspectives

Many times, I took notes alongside black parents as they sat in meetings with the principal to share their perceptions of the school and the areas where they wanted to see improvement. At one particular school, both parents and teachers complained that there was no honor roll or recognition of student academic achievement at the school—no assembly, no lunch with the principal, not even a display board for student academic honors. This was because the school had a particularly "diverse" population and thought an honor roll would be divisive, because the white and higher income students would be the ones who mostly received honors. To avoid conflict, there had been no honor roll for at least a decade.

A black mother and a white teacher had been talking regularly about the issue. Since I was the Teaching for Change lead at the school, they asked me to help them approach the principal and other parents. I recalled hearing many of the black parents and caregivers at the school, especially from lower income households, make comments like, "We had the honor roll when I was growing up, why don't we have anything like that here? I remember we used to get a pizza lunch, certificates, and had our names up in the hall." I worked with the lead parent and teacher to come up with an equitable plan and an approach that would engage people across the school community, particularly the black parents and caregivers from lower income households, the largest demographic in the school. Teachers were just as excited as parents about the program—they wanted something schoolwide to encourage their students to strive for, beyond their classroom celebrations.

Parents gave some initial input and then teachers drafted a plan, presenting two more drafts for feedback. "We think this should be based on grades, not on the testing," parents largely agreed. "And we want the awards to include the specials—art, PE, music, science, not just English and math." The result was the academic stars program, which included an honor roll based on grades, and an "on-a-roll" recognizing students who did not make the honor roll but whose grades had significantly improved. All of the academic stars were honored at a highly attended school assembly with certificates. At the awards ceremony, the teacher commented that the more they included parent voices, the more inclusive the program became, and that "made a big difference."

School-Based Parent Centers

Some of the most impactful moments I have seen and the fondest memories I have from schools come from seemingly ordinary moments. I have spent countless hours visiting parent centers at the DC schools I work with, and admittedly it took me a couple of years before I could recognize and appreciate how gatherings of black parents become exchanges of social and cultural capital. I learned a great deal as parents who were seemingly engaged in small talk about the world and their lives in actuality were exchanging vital information about how to stretch a dollar and how to access special education services and programs, housing vouchers, food and unemployment benefits, camps for their children, transportation assistance, and other necessities and enrichments to nurture their families' and children's needs and potential.

"Did you say your child is having a hard time in math? You know the red building next to the church on the next block? They have a free tutoring program, and my friend's son got a lot of help there."

I sat somberly with black parents as they exchanged the latest news about violence in their neighborhood, and used the eight-by-ten-foot room set aside as a parent center to grieve, heal, and talk about how they can protect their kids and their community. I argued with black parents over football games—especially after the rivalry games—and laughed every time someone shared a funny story, because the world communicates to black and poor parents that they do not deserve joy. In the midst of poverty, stress, budget cutting, overworked teachers, subpar conditions, the challenges of parenting, and overt racism and classism, schools can be spaces that embrace and engage the full humanity of our families rather than denying them.

Schools need black families at the table to meet the social, emotional, and academic needs of black students. For too long, public schools have institutionally pushed black families away and blamed them for the impacts that structural racism and classism can have on student performance. There is a rich field of knowledge about family engagement that educators can tap into to effectively engage black families. Engaging black families must move to the forefront of good teaching practices, and it must come with systemic supports and investments. Good intentions by individual teachers will get us to a point, and coupled with institutional knowledge and investments we can finally tap into one of the key ingredients for student and school success.

Our black students—and their families—are worth it.

Notes

1. Karen Mapp, Ilene Carver, and Jessica Lander, *Powerful Partnerships: A Teacher's Guide to Engaging Families for Student Success* (2017).

2. E. Ho Sui-Chu and J. D. Willms (1996) "Effects of parental involvement on eighth grade achievement," *Sociology of Education* 69 (2).

3. Karen Mapp, Ilene Carver, and Jessica Lander, *Powerful Partnerships: A Teacher's Guide to Engaging Families for Student Success* (2017).

4. Anthony S. Bryk et al., (2010) *Organizing Schools for Improvement: Lessons from Chicago* (Chicago: University of Chicago Press).

5. Endnote 8 from UNCF report "Done to Us, Not With Us: African American Parent Perceptions of K–12 Education" (2012).—O.C. Moles, (Ed.) (2000). *Reaching all families: Creating family-friendly schools, beginning of school year activities*. US Department of Education.

6. Soo Hong chapter in *A Chord of Three Strands* (2011).

7. Anne T. Henderson, Karen L. Mapp, Vivian R. Johnson, and Don Davies, *Beyond the Bake Sale* (2007); Karen Mapp, Ilene Carver, and Jessica Lander, *Powerful Partnerships: A Teacher's Guide to Engaging Families for Student Success* (2017).

8. *Between Families and Schools*, Teaching for Change, edited by Allyson Criner Brown (2016).

Who Do I Belong To?
A Black Teacher's Dilemma

Natalie Labossiere

Natalie Labossiere is a high school teacher in Beaverton, Oregon.

MY NINTH-GRADE GLOBAL STUDIES STUDENTS WERE PREPARING ARGU-ments for a trial role play for their semester final. After going over the day's expectations, I released them into groups to finish writing. I stopped and checked in with each group while walking around the classroom to discuss the direction they were taking with their presentations. After conferencing with a few students, I walked over to Izabel, Jalen, Alex, and Camila's table.

"How is it going?" I asked. "Real good, Ma'am," Jalen replied while giving me his typical mischievous smile. Jalen, an African American student who recently transferred from another area high school, is technically a tenth grader but was placed in my class for credit recovery. Despite transferring during the last two weeks of the semester, Jalen has been fearless as he has settled into my class. While he refused to do any work, he was charming and personable, and was willing to raise his hand and answer a question within his first five minutes in my class.

"All right," I responded. "Don't forget: your defenses need to be completed and typed for the role play by our next class."

Remembering that I had brought in a snack for the students to munch on while writing, I placed a tub of cookies in the middle table of the room. "Class, I brought in the cookies you like as a treat." I immediately stepped away because these students usually get very excited when I bring in snacks. Unsurprisingly, several students raced to the cookies.

Walking over to my computer, I heard Jalen shout, "Damn, nigger!" and I quickly looked up. Jalen looked upset and was glaring at Colin who was walking to his table with a fistful of cookies. I surveyed the room—Ellen, Jake, and Riley were opening their notebooks; Jace, whose face was bright red, was deliberately putting something in his bag; but pretty much the rest of the class was looking at me in disbelief. "Excuse me?" I asked the whole class, despite knowing exactly who had said it. "My bad," Jalen responded. "Yes, that was your bad," I replied, following up with "I do not want to hear that word used again."

Head down, Jalen walked back to his table and glanced at me as he sat. At this point I was anxious. I felt strongly that my brief reprimand of Jalen was not enough for him and the other students in the classroom, but I realized that how I needed to deal with Jalen individually was in direct conflict with how I needed to address the class. As an African American teacher in an affluent, suburban, predominantly white school, I was torn. If I publicly continued to reprimand Jalen, I knew I would be fracturing the new teacher-student relationship we had established. If I used this as a teachable moment to lead a class discussion, I would be using Jalen's words as the platform, which would hurt him, as it was evident that he was trying desperately to fit in. But I also wanted to give Jalen the opportunity to just be himself. As it is, African Americans are already required to assess and adjust continually in our daily lives. Everything we do is under intense scrutiny, and often they bear the brunt of an unusual amount of code switching from home to school. Shouldn't school be the one place Jalen doesn't have to change the way he talks?

I looked over at Jalen, and while he was in discussion with his group, he periodically looked over to me, checking to see if I was looking at him, and if I was angry with him.

To add to this difficulty, I understood him. I knew why he had said it, how he was feeling, and what he meant. I am fully aware of the historical racist context behind the N-word but within the African

American community and among my friends, this is a word we feel comfortable using with one another, but only with one another. Looking at Jalen I knew he did not understand this. To be one of a few is lonely. To be the "only" someone or something is frustrating. To be the only African American student in a class with a completely different socioeconomic makeup from yours can be just too much. I was already worried about him. He was such a sweet kid, but I was not sure whether he understood the intricacies of navigating a privileged, predominantly white school and I was afraid he was getting lost in the process. The school he had transferred from, Milwaukie High School, served a largely working-class community in suburban Portland—these two schools couldn't be more different. I had heard rumors of his behavior at his last school, but as I stated to him after welcoming him on his first day, a new school meant a new opportunity to start with a clean slate.

Feeling the need to do or say something, I struggled with the questions: Who did I belong to at that moment? Who was I there for? Who should I support?

Publicly reprimanding Jalen and having a class discussion on the N-word could have led to an understanding that these ninth graders desperately needed. It could have been the opportunity to discuss the historical context and related contemporary issues. I also was concerned that the classroom culture we had created had somehow been altered, but at the same time I felt that at that moment, I belonged to Jalen. I needed to let him know that his use of the word was inappropriate and I was disappointed in him, while reassuring him that he and I were still good.

I looked over at Jalen one more time, and he quickly turned away when I caught his eye. "Jalen, can we talk outside?"

"Laboss, I am sorry but there is nothing wrong with that word," he said as soon as we were standing outside of the class.

"Jalen, I got you and totally understand, but you should not have said it."

"Fine, I am sorry. I won't say that word in your class anymore," he said, looking down at the floor.

"This is bigger than my class. You can't say that word anymore because you just let a whole bunch of white students feel comfortable hearing that word and that is not okay."

I wanted him to realize the power he had in his words and actions.

"Man, everyone is always talking about how we should not say it, but there's nothing wrong with it, rappers say it all the time and have you seen that show *The Boondocks*? They say it all of the time. It's a term of affection."

"Huh?" I looked at him with disbelief. His argument made it clear that while he understood the different ways the N-word could be used, he clearly did not get the code regarding where and with whom.

"Were you trying to be affectionate with Colin?" I asked.

"Nah, that nigger was grabbing all of the cookies."

Feeling at this point that we were going in circles, I quickly nodded at my instructional aide to let her know this talk was going to be a bit longer and I asked Jalen to walk with me.

"Where we going?"

I reassured him that he was not in trouble and told him that I just wanted him to walk around the school with me. I felt I needed some reinforcement and hoped that we would run into Marcus. Marcus is the campus security supervisor at my high school and the only African American male staff member in a building of 2,500 students and about 300 teachers, administrators, and staff. His easy-going, no-nonsense attitude made him popular with our students. Not disappointing, we ran into Marcus while he was walking out of a classroom.

"Hi, what's up?" I asked.

Marcus looked back and forth between the two of us and responded, "Nothing much," while patting Jalen on the back.

As the three of us walked back toward my classroom, I realized that I needed to wrap this up as I had been away from my class for some time.

"Marcus, we just had an incident in the classroom where Jalen called someone the N-word."

"You did what?" Marcus raised his voice while stepping closer to Jalen. "Nah, man, you can't do that in this building."

"You guys are tripping. I told Laboss ain't nothing wrong with it," said Jalen, who was becoming increasingly frustrated.

"Man, look into the classroom," Marcus said, while pulling him closer to the window that looks into my class. "How many Black people do you see?"

"None," Jalen responded, looking down.

"Exactly," said Marcus. Interrupting, I asked, "How would you feel if they called you that word?" and Marcus added, "How would you feel if they said that to me or Laboss?"

Jalen responded softly: "I would have to punch them in their face."

"Exactly," Marcus said.

"Like I said, Jalen, I get you but you can't say that word around here because these other kids don't understand that they do not have a right to say it, and when you say it in my room you are making it okay."

Marcus added, "You are putting both of us in a really bad place and you can't do that because we are here to look out for you."

Feeling that we had made some gains with him, I jokingly told him to get back to class and get some cookies. Marcus and I silently shook our heads while giving each other looks of frustration, agreement, and satisfaction.

Teachers of color have difficult experiences working in predominantly white schools. On any given day, we may have to make decisions that force the question "who do we belong to" at that particular moment. We have to make these decisions because the needs of many may conflict with the needs of one. As an African American teacher, I do not want my students of color to walk away feeling that my class was just another class that left them feeling invisible. It would be great to say that as teachers, we give all of our students 100 percent of ourselves every single day. But at times, my students of color need reassurance or direction on how to operate in a predominantly white building. I care for all of my students, but at times I just belong to one.

I did not have a classroom discussion about the use of the N-word.

To My Sons' Future Teacher, Colleague, Sister/Brother, Co-madre, Maestra, Comrade, Friend

Crystal T. Laura

Crystal T. Laura is an assistant professor of educational leadership at Chicago State University. By day, she explores leadership preparation for learning in the context of social justice with the goal of teaching school administrators to recognize, understand, and address the school-to-prison pipeline. During the second shift, she co-parents two marvelous boys who give her work in the field of education particular urgency.

YOU CAN SEE THAT I'M ALREADY UNCERTAIN—HESITANT ABOUT HOW TO address you, unsure about who we are and who we might become to one another. I'll admit that at this moment I'm a bit anxious, partly because I'll surely make some wrong assumptions writing to you now and perhaps I'll overstep or misspeak. My anxiety runs much, much deeper and wider than that—it's shaded with dread and flecked with fear—but I'll come to that further along. For now I want to put my doubts and worries to the side, plunge in and start a dialogue with you in the hope that if I speak plainly with the possibility of being heard and listen mindfully with the possibility of being changed we will find or create our common ground. Let's begin this school-family connection straightaway.

My name is Crystal Laura, Zachary and Logan's mom. I start there because that identity—Mom—has been defining and all-consuming from the moment Zachary stepped into our world, eight years ago. Logan put the exclamation point on it five years later, and I've been rockin' the mom vibe ever since. So, defining, yes, but all-consuming probably overstates the case. I'm also a daughter, a sister, and partner, too. I am a Black woman.

I wake up every day thankful that I'm Black and breathing. A lot of Americans make the easy assumption—without much thought, with absolutely no effort—that their lives matter, but too many folks aren't so sure, and in fact the evidence—school funding, forced racial segregation, health outcomes, overrepresentation in prisons and jails—points to the reality that in the normal workings of the system, some lives are unimportant and even disposable. So, yes, I wake up grateful, and more than that, I wake up pleased and maybe a bit euphoric that my beautiful, energetic boys are Black and breathing. You may think I'm dramatizing or exaggerating, but I'm not. I know precisely what they risk being Black boys here in twenty-first-century America.

For all of that and more, I don't take anything for granted, and while it pisses me off and offends me, yes, indeed, I'm glad to be Black and breathing. In addition to mothering my boys, I teach teachers and principals in the College of Education at Chicago State University. As part of my university work, I travel often to lecture and lead professional development trainings on critical issues in urban education. Recently, I left the boys for a couple of days to spend time with older youth—kids of fifteen and sixteen, who live in New York City, on Rikers Island.

The name precedes it. Rikers Island covers 413 acres of land in the middle of the East River between Queens and the Bronx, adjacent to the runways of LaGuardia Airport. Sitting on that land is a complex of jails—ten of them. It is one of the world's largest correctional institutions—it's a penal colony, really—and from what I hear, it's one of the world's worst, too. It is notorious for the abuse and neglect of people who are locked up there. You might remember the story that surfaced a couple of years ago about Kalief Browder, who was falsely accused of stealing a backpack, refused to plead out, and couldn't afford bail. He spent three years on Rikers waiting for a trial that never happened—two of those three years in solitary confinement—and he was so deeply impacted by his experiences there that two full years after he left the Island, and after Jay Z and Rosie O'Donnell and others donated materials and funds to get his life back in order, he hung himself.

There are over eleven thousand other men, women, and children on Rikers—the youngest of them are mandated to attend school. That means that we also have colleagues on Rikers—general grade-level teachers, special education teachers, counselors, social workers, paraprofessionals, principals, and district staff—who work with incarcerated students behind the walls.

I was invited to Rikers, as I am to other prisons and jails—places I've come to regard as sites of congealed violence—on the strength of a book I wrote called *Being Bad: My Baby Brother and the School-to-Prison Pipeline*. The book was born of love for my brother Chris, and rage at all the circumstances—self-inflicted and close to home as well as system-generated and as predictable as rain—that landed Chris in Illinois state prison doing a six-year bid.

On the first day of the visit, I toured the school sites on Rikers—sat in on classes, met with young people, asked the adults some questions, really became a student of that place—and then on the second day, I gave a reflective talk to our colleagues about what I learned. What I told them was this: without question, our current systems need a complete overhaul; but, in the meantime, they can work wonders—what one counselor called acting as a "cool drink of water in hell"—and with proper values and education, a strong network of support, and a whole lot of conviction, they can make great strides toward rethinking, reimagining, redesigning altogether how we approach harm, healing, and justice.

I see you, my sister/teacher and my sons' future teacher, like I saw them, as a cool drink of water in what is, quite frankly, for some young people, hell. I want us to put our heads together about how to better understand and radically shift the hellish contexts within which too many students find themselves marginalized and dismissed, and placed deliberately on the road to perdition.

I wonder if you know that, as a teacher, you are either engaged in incarceration prevention or incarceration expansion. It's just that real.

Because here and now, in the twenty-first century, we are seeing and experiencing an age of mass incarceration, a time when the prison is our go-to mechanism of isolation and containment, the central way that we adjudicate disputes, and the primary site where we deal with social trauma and social dilemmas.

Right now 1 in 31 American adults is under some form of correctional control—meaning incarcerated, on parole, or on probation: 1 in every 31. There are over two million men and women locked up in the United States—including my twenty-three-year-old brother—and besides the extraordinary number of incarcerated people, an even bigger problem is that we think that's normal. America of 2016 is a place that confines more of our people than any other country in the world, more Black adults than were enslaved in 1850. This is the contemporary context, and I wonder if you know that.[1]

But it's important for us, as educators, to stay alive to our expanding prison nation. Not just when somebody escapes and not only when we catch a marathon of those juicy, addictive documentaries—*Snapped*, *Drugs, Inc.*, *Lockdown*, or if you're old-school, *Cops*. It's crucial for us to pay attention to prisons partly because our profession—and we—are parties to barricading people in them. It's true. On every measure of academic attainment—earning a diploma, a GED, or some form of postsecondary education—those who are incarcerated lag far behind those of us in the free world. They have lower literacy levels, fewer marketable skills, and a greater prevalence of mental and physical disabilities. With regard to education and schooling, incarcerated people are often those who, from us, once needed the most, and somehow got the least.

I wonder if you know that, and if you are keeping your eyes open wide to our current situation, which is largely defined by jails and prisons that are so full of Brown and Black bodies that most everyone who knows what I'm talking about and has good sense is practically begging schools to stop feeding them.

I want to say a bit about the school-to-prison pipeline, because it strikes a special chord in me every time I meet someone—someone in the field of education, especially—who has never heard the phrase. I hope that uncomfortable, justice-oriented conversations are happening in your classes and in your school. But ask a classroom teacher, a director, a principal, a parent, or school board member who is not well-versed in critical issues of urban education or about the school-to-prison pipeline, and you can expect little more than a polite nod and smart use of context clues. I'm just saying. No offense, I've gotten that "I don't know what you're talking about, but something tells me I should" response more than a few times.

I often assume that the problem is one of semantics. Let's be honest, the term "school-to-prison pipeline" is not exactly part of everyday lingo, and even across activist circles the mind-blowing idea that kids get funneled from systems of education to systems of juvenile and criminal justice has actually been captured by a number of other nifty metaphors. Off the top, I can think of three: one is the "schoolhouse-to-jailhouse track," another is the "cradle-to-prison pipeline," and a third is the "school-prison nexus." All are school-to-prison pipeline derivatives, if you will, and each highlights the fact that our profession is hardly the great equalizer that it's hyped up to be. I want you to remember that schools and prisons are like close cousins, not twins—and this distinction is important, because if we're to dismantle the school-to-prison pipeline, which we will, then we've got to be clear about not only our language, but our deeper goals and how we're directing our efforts, and where to seek support from co-liberators.

For example, if you are deeply concerned about the ways in which school-based policies and practices help young people along to jails and prisons, then you have to take a look at reports published by the Advancement Project. The Advancement Project is a multi-racial civil rights organization founded by a team of lawyers who have taken on a variety of social issues, including redistricting, voter protection, immigrant justice, and the on-the-ground realities of "zero tolerance."

By now zero tolerance in our schools and workplaces is as common as dirt, but some of us are too young to remember how things got this way. In the early 1990s, there was a spike of juvenile homicides, then a resulting public panic, fueled by a racially coded media frenzy around teenage "superpredators," and then the passage of federal and state laws to mete them out—all of this could have easily gone over our heads. But the staff at the Advancement Project, and others, started putting out reports that really help us understand what it means when school adults have "zero tolerance" for children and youth in their buildings.

As absolute as zero tolerance sounds, we aren't equally intolerant of all kids. Of course, I won't argue that we should be, but why is it that poor students, students of color, LGBTQ students, and students with disabilities so frequently get the short end of the stick?

I remember one spring semester I taught a teacher education course on urban education policy, and the topic of "bad kids" emerged as a particular favorite among my students. Most everyone wanted to know how to run a tight ship, stay sane, and keep safe with so many "troublemakers" and "class clowns" in Chicago public schools. Whenever I pushed people to unpack the beliefs embedded within this kind of philosophy and everyday language, things always got ugly. Public schools were equated with city schools, city kids with cultural poverty and dysfunction. The stock stories commodified by the mainstream media—the news, Hollywood films, cable network television, and the music industry—about pathological and dangerous youth poured in. And the grapevine, with its salacious tales from the field, was tugged as proof positive that some children will inevitably fall through the cracks.

As lively as these discussions were, no one ever seemed to want to talk about the connections between how we think and talk about children and how we treat them in social and academic contexts. A hush usually fell over the crowd when I suggested that demonizing ideology and discourse enables a whole web of relationships, conditions, and social processes—a social ecology of discipline—which works on and through the youth who rub against our understanding of "good" students. Granted, these were young, pre-service teachers who had very little, if any, direct experience with children in urban schools. So, I'm guessing that part of their silence was rooted in ignorance. It's also true though that challenging and unlearning what we assume we know about people, places, and things is uncomfortable, and that finagling around contradictions and tensions of implicit and explicit bias is easier than diving into and grappling with them. But that's exactly what we educators ought to be doing, diving into the wreckage.

Because if we don't, we will continue to build schools like "Rosa Parks Elementary," a fake name for a real place, where educational researcher Ann Ferguson found that Black male students of ten and eleven years old were routinely and openly described by school adults as "at risk" of failing, "unsalvageable," and "bound for jail."[2] Help me out here: sticks and stones may break my bones, but what? Words will never hurt me. Bullshit, yes they will.

Because when our perceptions are so profoundly distorted that we can think and talk about our students in these ways, then we have no trouble acting accordingly. In a room of thirty students, with precious few resources to go around, and with the alphabet soup of standardized tests never far away—we have no space, no patience, zero tolerance for "misbehavior." The problem, of course, is that what counts as "misbehavior" depends.

Black boys, for example, are often refracted through cultural images of Black males as both dangerous and endangered, and their transgressions are sometimes framed as different from those of other children. Black boys are what Ann Ferguson calls "doubly displaced"—meaning that as Black children, they are not seen as childlike, but "adultified"; their misdeeds are "made to take on a sinister, intentional, fully conscious tone that is stripped of any element of childish naivete."[3] As Black males, they are often denied the masculine dispensation that White male students get as being "naturally naughty"; instead, Black boys are discerned as willfully bad.[4]

So we put them out of class and out of school. We suspend them. We punish them excessively, usually for minor offenses, like talking about a Hello Kitty bubble gun, hugging a friend, and chewing a Pop-Tart into the shape of a gun. In Chicago, where I live and work, zero tolerance policies in the district's schools were abolished in 2006 in favor of restorative justice approaches to harm and healing, but still the number of suspensions has nearly doubled since then. Black boys in my hometown are five times more likely to be suspended than any other group of students in the city's public school system. Black boys comprise 23 percent of the district's student population, but amount to 44 percent of those who are suspended, and 61 percent of those who are expelled. Black boys are the only group of Chicago Public School students whose suspension rates are higher in elementary school than in high school.

Chicago has its issues. Chicago is the epicenter of neoliberal school reform, the third-largest school district in the country, and one of the few without an elected school board. We've had over a hundred neighborhood school closures since 2001 and an eightfold increase in money going to charters. One hundred twenty-six schools don't have libraries. You know what, don't get me started. School politics in Chicago is for another letter.

Let's be clear—wherever you work or live likely has its issues, too. But the problem is much bigger than where we work because when we have zero tolerance for our kids, we not only suspend them, but we expel them. We not only suspend and expel them, but we arrest them—in schools, not only do we have cops or school resource officers on deck (as we saw in South Carolina), we've constructed booking stations in the school buildings to make school-based arrests easier, faster, and more efficient.

When we have zero tolerance for our kids, we lose all concept of kids being kids—wiggling, jumping, giggling, fidgeting somehow gets diagnosed and labeled and medicated.

And when that doesn't work, we beat them. Yes, beat them—with canes, straps, paddles, and yardsticks. Corporal punishment is still allowed in twenty states.

When we have zero tolerance for kids and their "misbehavior," we even fine them. Back home, a single network of charter schools collects about $200K annually from student discipline fees—$5 per infraction for things like missing a button on your shirt or being seen with a bag of chips—add that to the revenue from a summer behavior class at $140 per registrant and you've got yourself a promising fundraiser on the backs of the poor, Black students, and their families.[5]

And if the kids for whom we have zero tolerance have not yet dropped out, we transfer them to other schools or counsel them toward programs like the Job Corps, which has been called the U.S. Department of Labor's boarding school for the "bottom of society" and what I would argue is an intermediary or pit stop in the schoolhouse-to-jailhouse track.

I could go on, but I think that you get the point, which is that these school policies and practices are systems of surveillance, exercises of power used to continuously and purposefully monitor poor youth and youth of color.[6] I am a Black woman, a mother of two beautiful Black sons, so you'll understand why I am particularly attuned to the ways that schools wound Black boys. Black boys are unevenly punished and tracked into educational disability categories in their early years, practices that tend to reinforce the very problems they intend to correct. And although this is enough to make reasonable people want to holler, even more insidious is when those under surveillance internalize the experiences and labels assigned to them, when they believe the exclusion and isolation has been defensible, and when they learn to condition themselves. Then Black boys who have been sorted, contained, and pushed out of schools become Black men—men whose patterns of hardship are pronounced and deeply entrenched, who constitute more than one-third of the adult males in prison and are six times more likely than white men to be incarcerated—men who have been well primed for neither college, career, nor full participation in our democracy, but instead for punitive institutionalization.[7]

If you are moved by this—this brief description of how school policies and practices nudge some youth toward dropout—then I hope you'll consider grounding your approach to teaching in dismantling the school-to-prison pipeline, and in reframing your work in such a way that the school is not a place of punishment, that the school doesn't label more people ID and LD than it does PhD and JD, that the school is not the primary gateway to degrading labor, the streets, and permanent detention. I think your job is to yearn for and create the kinds of classrooms and schools that folks don't need to recover from. I want you to look at your position as disrupting the school-to-prison pipeline and as engaging in anti-prison work. And I think we can agree that a classroom that foregrounds love, justice, and joy is where we can begin—and where we will begin again.

I am happy to support you in this endeavor. All love, All/ways.

Notes

1. Michelle Alexander, *The New Jim Crow: Mass Incarceration in the Age of Colorblindness* (New York: The New Press, 2012), 180.

2. Ann Arnett Ferguson, *Bad Boys: Public Schools in the Making of Black Masculinity* (Ann Arbor: University of Michigan Press, reprint, 2001).

3. Ferguson, *Bad Boys*, 83.

4. Ferguson, *Bad Boys*, 80.

5. Traci G. Lee, "Chicago Charter Schools Rake in Thousands in 'Disciplinary Fees,'" Melissa Harris-Perry/Education on MSNBC, January 3, 2013, http://www.msnbc.com/melissa-harris-perry/chicago-charter-schools-rake -thousands.

6. Michel Foucault, *Discipline & Punish: The Birth of the Prison*, rev. ed. (Gallimard, in French, 1975; New York: Vintage Books, 1995).

7. E.A. Carson, *Prisoners in 2016*, Washington, DC: Bureau of Justice Statistics, 2018, https://www.sentencingproject.org/wp-content/uploads/2016/01 /Trends-in-US-Corrections.pdf.

Gender and
Sex Ed Matter

Sexual Harassment and the Collateral Beauty of Resistance

Camila Arze Torres Goitia

Camila Arze Torres Goitia teaches at Madison High School in Portland, Oregon. She is the author of "Colonizing Wild Tongues," which was published in the summer 2015 issue of Rethinking Schools.

"WE HAVE SOMETHING TO TELL YOU, BUT WE'RE WORRIED ABOUT GET-ting you too involved. We don't want to get you in trouble," Baylee and Zaida whispered excitedly as they wiggled through the crack in my classroom door on my prep. I was confused to see them in such high spirits because earlier in the day they had been crushed by news from our administration. For more than two months they had been part of our Restorative Justice Club that had been planning two half-day workshops around women empowerment for female-identifying students and toxic masculinity for male-identifying students. The club of eleven demographically diverse students had been urging adults in our building to do something about sexual harassment since October when they made sexual assault and harassment their Restorative Justice Club theme of the month and visited freshman classes to lead circles on the topic. This opened up a door for freshmen to continue to reach out to upperclassmen about the harassment they were facing.

The issues were metastasizing and students hoped to get to the heart of the matter with the two workshops that would explore sexualization, intersectionality, and slut-shaming. They scheduled the workshops for January to give themselves enough time to plan, and for two months and even over winter break, they worked tirelessly to put them together: sending invitations, making lesson plans, collaborating with strong teacher leaders who gave advice and feedback along the way. This is why they were so devastated to hear from our administration just one week before the scheduled workshops that they had to be postponed because students just could not afford to miss a class or two a couple weeks before finals.

No one seemed more upset than Baylee and Zaida, who had been impacted by Madison High School's strong curriculum on sex trafficking their sophomore year in health class and carried on the fire for the next year and a half. So when they walked in right before the last bell, I knew they were going to come at me with that same urgency.

"Administration is obviously not listening to us and our needs and sexual harassment has been a big problem since, like, yesterday, so we're just going to protest," Baylee said. Mixed emotions of excitement and fear bubbled up in me. It was the moment I wait for every year: seeing students believe in themselves as agents of change and feeling empowered to act on something they care about. It is the aim of our Social Studies team at Madison to lift up resistance to injustice and provide models for fighting back. Still, I would be lying if I said I wasn't scared as a kerosene cat in hell when the moment finally came marching through my door at 3:13 p.m. on a Friday.

For the past few months, our school had been dealing with a plague that crept through our hallways and classrooms and was infecting students' social media accounts. At the beginning of the year, a four-foot, eleven-inch-tall seventeen-year-old Latinx student had been pushed into a bookshelf when she ignored her male classmate in class. That same week a few freshmen had come forward about upperclassmen offering $5 to anyone who "slapped that fast freshman ass" referring to what they saw as the new "crop" of ninth-grade girls. A month later, it came out that a student had cornered a girl in an empty hallway and ran his hand up her thigh. At our talent show, an openly gay African American student and king of dance had homophobic and sexualized remarks posted about him and his dance routine on Snapchat. In the hallways, boys were taking away girls' cellphones saying they wouldn't give them back until the girls let the boys follow them on social media, or worse, until the girls would "suck their dick." It became difficult for females to walk down the stairs without someone staring up their skirts, or up the stairs without someone commenting on their "baddie asses." Nonconsensual pictures were popping up on secret Instagram accounts of girls, trans-boys, and gay boys with pink and lime-green free-drawn penises next to their faces. A few freshman girls transferred classes and, in some cases, schools to avoid condoms thrown at them in class—"to be used on them later"—or rulers shimmying up their shirts.

It was not that the administration was not listening to these cases or attempting to address the ones that girls felt safe enough to report. The problem was that all their efforts were obviously not working, and they were relying on the one tiny paragraph on sexual harassment in our school district policy for guidance. For many students, it felt like sexual harassment was occurring with impunity. Some perpetrators received only half-day suspensions, and when asked what they learned from them, they blithely replied, "I got to sleep in today." Clearly, more had to be done.

Every time I share these incidents with folks outside the Madison community, they seem shocked. "Wow, your school is so broken," "Your school is a mess," "That's so crazy that it's gotten that bad at your school." If this year has taught the world anything, it is that our school is not an anomaly. This year we have seen folks of all gender identities from all across the country and world say "#MeToo," we have seen the strength and courage it takes to call out behaviors so pervasive and ingrained in our society, and we have seen perpetrators from Harvey Weinstein to Matt Lauer condemned.

But we have also seen what goes unaddressed and unpunished. At the national level we have seen what seems to be countless women come forward with allegations against the supposed "leader of the free world" with no consequence. And at the local level my students know that communities of color (like theirs) face multiple barriers when dealing with the aftermath of sexual harassment, assault, and violence. Students pick up on this. The only difference between sexual harassment at Madison and sexual harassment at other schools is that students started naming the behaviors that have been ravaging high schools for years, reporting them, and sharing their stories with each other.

I guess the weight of the issue and the strength of the victims who were coming forward beat out fear for my job security that day. So, when Baylee and Zaida asked if they could use our RJ Club meeting space and time to reach out to people who might want to be involved, I took a risk and gave them my room. Over the next two weeks, the Restorative Justice Club hosted three meetings and came up with a plan of action.

Our regular RJ meetings usually consisted of around five to seven students, myself, and our school RJ coordinator/champion, Nyanga. I was pleasantly surprised to see twenty-one students pulling up chairs and forming an amoeba of a circle during the first meeting, during which the RJ Club sent out invites to possible allies and leaders they thought capable of changing minds and hearts around the school.

I stepped outside for a bit after introductions, still trying to balance wanting to protect myself with the absolute inability to contain my excitement over what was evolving in my room. Outside my door, I ran into Ryan Ghan locking up the computer lab and whispered to him, "I think something big is happening in my room. Students may protest against sexual harassment." Ryan, a thoughtful and bighearted teacher who had done a lot to model collaboration and delegation in my first few years of teaching, had just helped with the rejuvenation of our school's Feminist Club, which had fizzled out over intersectionality disputes the year before. He immediately responded, "That's awesome. It sounds like I should go get Feminist Club?" Bless his heart, because within ten minutes, twenty-one turned into thirty-five. Feminist Club and RJ Club combined their powers, Captain Planet–style, through social media posts, hand-delivered invites, and word-of-mouth: There were close to sixty participants at the next two planning sessions. By the third and final meeting, the room was packed with the usual suspects but also a large group of trans-men who had just seen a social media post a couple of days before made by a Madison student saying, "I'll fuck up any faggot who walks into Madison." There were also four African American football players who were starting to question the toxic masculinity perpetuated by some of their teammates and, at times, themselves. There was a big group from our Latinx student club that had held the weight of machismo on their shoulders and weren't afraid to spit knowledge about it whenever the room seemed white-dominated. And there was a chunk of our Muslim Student Alliance that was still outraged about a girl's hijab being ripped off during PE the year before. Everyone had a story and the levels of "me toos" echoing around the room moved the three adults sitting in the corner, watching and listening, who didn't do much except bring pizza to fuel the revolution.

As students started to organize and get down to the nitty-gritty of planning over the course of their three meetings, I found myself wanting to ask questions or tell them what they had to do. Bad teaching moves, to be sure. Luckily, the adults in the room held our tongues long enough to discover that every single concern we had would be swiftly addressed within a minute by a student. When I started to worry that students didn't have a clear purpose, they came up with demands. When I started to worry that they didn't have a plan of action for what to do based on administration or security's reactions, they created a multiple-scenario script on what leaders should say should they come into conflict. When voices started to dominate, they opened up the conversation. Students showed me over the next two weeks of planning that, when community is at stake, students are capable of anything.

"Whatever We Wear, Wherever We Go, Yes Means Yes, No Means No!"

As the Feminist Club students filed into my classroom during that first meeting, Baylee repeated the purpose: "We basically wanted to protest because we think sexual harassment is a really big problem and we're not being listened to." She, Zaida, and De'ja (another RJ Club member) went on to explain how their event to educate and take action around sexual harassment was cancelled. "This is a problem right now and I think the only way they're going to see that is if we show them by protesting or walking out," Zaida concluded. Faisal, a young Muslim student always in for a good cause, asked, "Do you think it would be more powerful for us to all walk out together or to all sit in a part of the school and chant or something? Because I feel like if we walk out they might just ignore us." During that and the other two meetings, I saw students weigh their options carefully and with conviction, ensuring all students in the room were seen and heard.

"I think we should be united and civilized like the Black Panthers," Baylee said, referencing a strong civil rights curriculum she received from our Feminist Club co-advisor, Ken Gadbow. "We should all wear black and stand together with a clear message," Zaida added. "We need demands like in Soweto," added a sophomore student who remembered our Modern World History team's South African apartheid unit from his freshman year. The students landed on the idea of a sit-in but worried about how to recruit members to join and keep the space inclusive.

"Picture this: We split up into different sections in the school in the morning and march so we can recruit people who are in the hallways going to class," said a young student who had had experiences with protests in the Portland area. "Maybe we can make up a chant in the hallways so people know what we're marching for?" said a senior athlete. "Or make a pamphlet or half sheet with our demands," Baylee interjected. "I think we need to find a way to get more people of color at our meetings," the co-president of La Raza Unida said as she noticed just three Latinx students in the room. She went to her club meeting the next day and urged all club members to join.

"We need to make protest posters, for sure, and I can do that after school this week. Who can get some poster board?" one of them said at the next meeting. "They always have leftover cardboard in the library," suggested a library TA who always helped with our culturally relevant library displays and is transgender. Worried about low participation due to semester finals around the corner and inspired by the action at the 2018 Golden Globes to raise awareness of women working low-wage jobs who've been sexually harassed or assaulted, students also started posting pictures of the related Time's Up logo on their Instagram accounts with a caption asking everyone to wear black on the day of the action against sexual harassment and assault (January 17) and to "DM me for more information on how to get involved."

We ask students to be supportive group members in class so often. We ask them to check in on their group mates, to help them get un-stuck, to listen to others' ideas, to not miss class and leave their group hanging. Sometimes it works beautifully and other times it's disas-trous (is that just in my classroom?), and I think we're never quite sure how that lesson lands with our students. What I saw over the course of just a few meetings was students getting to each meeting on time, planning carefully, collaborating wholeheartedly, and mak-ing the best of the resources at hand. By the end of their last meeting, their demands were written and the plan was set:

1. Actual consequences put on perpetrators of sexual harassment.
2. A clear, written policy on sexual harassment now from ad-ministrators and a plan to prevent it by February 7.
3. A written statement from Portland Public Schools by Feb-ruary 17 stating how they will protect students and create a more supportive environment for victims. We demand to know what actions they will take and how they will take ac-countability for their neglect of these situations.

They would march from the cafeteria where there would be a crowd of students getting breakfast and through the social studies hallway where they felt they had the most teacher allies. They would chant, "Whatever we wear, wherever we go, yes means yes, no means no!"

The Talking Stick: Lip Gloss

At 8 a.m. on January 17, excitement was unbelievably high for so early in the morning, as students filled up the C-crossroads—a fancy name for a wide hallway in the middle of our school's second floor—and their chants echoed through the school. The hallways were alive as teachers and students peered out doorways and, in some cases, ran to the center of the school to join. At 8:21, students started to find their seats on the ground. Organizers had done a lot to prepare for this moment. They had written up a press statement and created a multiple-scenario script of pre-planned responses to administration, security, or students opposed to the sit-in. As the students started to settle on the ground, they started to look around for a leader.

"Alright everyone, we're going to be here for a while I hope, so let's talk," a student organizer said. As administrators and security popped in, seemingly unsure of how to respond and taking pictures occasionally, the most organic and exquisite restorative justice circle commenced. For seven hours, there would be a constant presence of well over a hundred students seated in a circle in our main hallway sharing their stories and concerns. Some students joined for just one class period or for a fifteen-minute "bathroom break" while others stayed the whole day. A good number of teachers came to listen, learn, and witness our courageous students following the restorative justice practices our school had prioritized since our current seniors' freshman year. The talking stick: lip gloss. The centerpiece: student protest posters. The theme: students' demands and stories. The rest grew from there. Students raised their hands if they wanted the lip gloss in order to speak and listened with a full heart to some harrowing tales of harassment and inspiring ideas for prevention. When disagreements came up, they were addressed with an incredible level of respect and maturity. When a young African American freshman said she didn't want her younger sister "dressing like a slut" while expressing the importance of being a good role model and teaching siblings better than to harass or assault, hands went up.

"I think I know what you're trying to say," one theater student started, "but I think a lot of people are uncomfortable with the word 'slut' because they don't want to be ashamed and it takes their own agency away. You and I should be able to dress however we choose and we should be shaming those who harass us or make us feel bad for that choice, you know what I'm saying?"

The freshman heard a few more stories and opinions on her word choice, and when I feared students were over-policing word choice and pushing out a student of color from their movement, she bravely stood up and asked for the lip gloss, apologized for the way her word choice landed, and restated her point without using the word again.

When a couple of students started naming perpetrators, Mitch, who had been tirelessly reaching out to media all week, urged us to follow the Madison-wide restorative justice norm of confidentiality during class circles. "It's important to name harassers in reports to the principals and stuff, but we should focus on our stories here and not name names." When the conversation turned female-dominated, a male Step Up advocate requested the lip gloss. "I think one thing we can do as men of color and anyone else, really, is to do what we're doing now. Have these conversations with our friends, our family. I have these talks with my friends all the time, and it's important to reflect and make sure we're being thoughtful in our interactions with girls." This call for self-reflection obviously landed well, as a little while later, a young Latinx male talked about a time when he wished he would have made a better choice and expressed gratitude for his brother who modeled positive relationships with women.

Sometimes there were disagreements. Sometimes students paused to teach each other what sexual harassment looks like ("Unwanted stares can be harassment, too! Some boys around here exoticize us hardcore," a young Vietnamese student said). And sometimes there were chilling stories, like when a sophomore girl was invited by an upperclassman to go to a convenience store over the weekend and was told she was going to be kicked out of the car unless she performed oral sex.

For seven hours, though, there was never a lull.

Celebration and Reflection

As the last bell rang and more than 120 students stood up and stretched their tired knees, organizers looked across the breaking circle at each other with pride. They had done it. Baylee sent me a text from across the hall asking if we could debrief in my class. We all plopped down on my couch and sighed. They had triumphed over trauma and made something beautiful out of something hard with the unwavering magic of their voices. Students went over their exciting meeting with administrators, and Nyanga congratulated them on their bravery and strength. I expected students to bask in the glory of their success: administrators were currently writing a statement and hashing out a policy that would be returned to students by the deadline imposed in their demands, and the head of our district high schools had heard their concerns. Students had won—our school had won.

Instead, they used this time to bring up things they wished they had done and hoped to do better next time. "Remember when Ivan had his hand up for, like, twenty minutes and a bunch of white girls got to speak before him?" Ivan is a Mexican American sophomore who, indeed, shook his head every time a "hipster" girl was called on before him. "Yeah, we need to be better at calling on people of color since they seemed less likely to speak in the circle," Baylee said. "Not because they didn't want to, but maybe just because they needed more wait time or something," De'ja added.

I was proud of my students for seeing the room for growth in their accomplishments while still heading to the bus at four p.m. with their heads held high, ready to see the change their sit-in brought to our community.

Believe Me the First Time

Dale Weiss

Dale Weiss has been a public school teacher for the past twenty-five years and is a frequent contributor to Rethinking Schools.

"I'M NOT A BOY! I'M A GIRL! I'M A GIRL! I'M A GIRL!" I FOLLOWED THE words echoing through my suddenly silent second-grade classroom. There sat Alexis on the floor with Diego; puzzle pieces were strewn across the floor.

"What's wrong, Alexis?" I asked. "You sound upset."

"Every day someone asks me if I am a boy or a girl, and every time I answer that I'm a girl, but they just keep asking. Why can't they believe me?"

I thought back to the many conversations I'd had with Alexis about this topic since the beginning of the school year. Alexis is a bright, confident child who expresses herself with ease. When I heard someone ask her if she was a boy or a girl, I would check in: "How do you feel when your classmates ask you about your gender?"

And each time her reply was pretty much the same. "I'm okay. It's not really their fault. They just didn't know."

Several times I asked Alexis if she thought it would be a good idea to discuss this issue as a class—not to call attention to her but to explore in general the issue of gender. Each time she responded: "No, I don't think we need to do that."

"Why not?" I once asked.

"Because it's not that big a deal."

I told Alexis that if she changed her mind, she should tell me, but I felt tugged in two directions. As a teacher, I frequently explore the "-isms" with my students (racism, classism, sexism, heterosexism, and so on) as a critical piece of teaching from an anti-bias perspective. At the same time, I wanted to respect Alexis's decision to hold off—though for how long, I was not sure.

Now I pulled Alexis aside. By this time she was in tears. "I tried to be patient with people. I said they were asking me because they didn't know. But I don't understand why they don't believe me when I say I am a girl. Why do they have to keep asking?"

As I gave Alexis a long hug, I thought about another student, one who'd been in my class two years prior. Classmates often expressed confusion as to whether Allie was a girl or a boy, too. And, as in Alexis's situation, classmates often did not accept her response. I flashed back to the time that year when we were discussing a story about children who wore uniforms to school. I'd asked my students if they would like to wear school uniforms. Allie's arm shot up in the air with fierce determination. "Yes! I would totally love it if kids wore uniforms in our school. That way all of us would be dressed the same and kids would finally stop asking me if I am a boy or a girl."

Alexis and I Plan a Teaching Unit

Back in the present, I said to Alexis: "I think it's time to deal with gender issues head-on with our class. Would you consider developing and leading a unit with me?" The tears were gone. "I sure would!"

The words spilled out of my mouth before I realized I'd offered to co-create a teaching unit with a student. I felt excited at the idea, but I'd never done it before. I often respond to issues and interests that emerge from my students by developing a unit—but collaborating with one of my students on creating and teaching a unit was definitely a first.

"How about if we meet after school on Wednesday? I'll check with your mom."

"Sure!"

By this point in the year, we'd already had numerous and ongo-ing discussions about ways to build a supportive community in our classroom—and how, when we make a mistake, we can repair harm with one another. So we had a context for talking about gender in ways that would support Alexis. She was well liked by her peers and accepted as an integral part of our classroom community. I did not believe Alexis's classmates were intentionally trying to bully her—they were genuinely confused about her gender identity. However, I wanted my students to understand that consistently questioning someone about their gender identity can be experienced as bullying.

A few days later, we began our collaboration. "Alexis, why don't you first look through the books in our classroom library and pull out anything that addresses issues of gender and accepting people for who they are."

Twenty minutes later she brought over her book selections. I was excited to look at her pile until I realized it consisted of only seven books.

"Were there any others, Alexis?"

"Nope, this was it."

When I looked through the books she brought me and thought about the books we had, I realized she was right. "Wow!" I exclaimed. "This sure doesn't seem like enough books when the topic of gender is so incredibly important." Definitely one of those teacher moments when I realized I needed to do far better.

Alexis had already read each of those seven books. I asked her what she enjoyed—or perhaps didn't enjoy—about the books.

"There's nothing I didn't enjoy. But what I did enjoy is that when I read these books, I felt accepted for who I am."

A few days later, Alexis ran up to me when she arrived at school. "Ms. Dale, I thought I'd bring you one of my books from home in case you want to read it." The book was *Meet Polkadot* by Talcott Broadhead.

"Tell me what the book's about, Alexis."

"This book is so cool! It's all about a person named Polkadot and how when they were born, they didn't get called any gender."

"And what do you like most about this book?"

"I like that the book celebrates whatever gender someone feels they are, and that it's all really okay! You can borrow the book if you'd like to."

"I'd love to, Alexis. Thank you for sharing this book with me." Now I knew that Alexis viewed herself as an integral participant in shaping our unit.

Alexis Finds a Fourth-Grade Mentor

In the meantime, I learned from a colleague that Allie, my former student, had been experiencing a lot of bullying from other fourth graders because of how she dressed. I wondered if I could help. I spoke with Allie's mom and asked her if Allie might be interested in the Peace Club I was running twice a week during recess and lunch. One of the Peace Club's topics was how to deal with bullying at our school. I asked Allie if she would like to be our fourth-grade mentor and she agreed. Allie and Alexis's brother had been friends since kindergarten.

During Allie's first session of the Peace Club, the students were making friendship bracelets. I sat down at an empty group of desks, only to be joined by two students who'd been up getting supplies: Allie and Alexis. I introduced them to each other. Alexis said: "I knew who you were because my brother is in your class. He told me you get bullied for the same things that I do." Then Alexis turned to me. "I have an idea! How about if Allie works on the gender project with us?"

I thought that was a great idea and asked Alexis to explain the project to Allie. And so our project expanded; we were now a group of three.

We met three more times before launching the gender unit in my second-grade class. First we talked about different ways to approach the issue. After the brainstorming, both Allie and Alexis spoke about ways they had experienced bullying. Alexis began:

Last summer I went to camp. On the registration form my parents said I was a girl. When I got to camp I waited in the check-in line with the other girls, but then this person who worked for the camp said I was in the wrong line. I tried to tell him that I was in the right line, but he kept arguing with me and showed me where they'd changed me to the boys' cabin. Finally it got worked out. But, in the meantime, all the other kids stared at me. I felt awful.

Allie listened intently, then shared her own story:

One time I went with my mom to a store to get some new clothes. We were in the boys department because that is where I can find the clothes that I like the best. This saleslady came up to us and asked if we needed help finding something. I told her I was looking for some shirts and pants. She said "For you?!" so loud that everybody in the whole store could hear. I said, "Yes, for me." Then she kept telling me I had to go into the girls department because I was in the wrong part of the store. I felt really, really bad. And so did my mom. We left the store and went someplace else.

"That must have been really awful."
"Yeah, it was."
Soon we began to map out our unit. I said that I often found it helpful, when beginning a new unit with students, to find out their beliefs and thoughts about the subject. "Perhaps we could begin by giving students different categories to think about and comment on. Clothes, for example: Which clothes do students think of as 'girls' clothes' or 'boys' clothes' or clothes that are worn by both girls and boys?"

Alexis excitedly piped in, "We could do a Venn diagram!" Allie and I both thought that was a great idea. At first we talked about two interlocking circles—one labeled *girls*, one labeled *boys*—with the overlapping space in the middle labeled *both*. Allie paused for a second and then said: "But I think there will be a problem if we do the circles like this. Won't the space called both need to be larger?"

Alexis chimed in: "I get what you're talking about. If we make the both space larger, that would kind of give away what we're thinking." Alexis and Allie then decided to make three equal-sized circles on a long piece of butcher paper: girls on one side, boys on the other, both in the middle. We brainstormed the categories we wanted students to think about: sports, games, toys, animals, music, colors, songs, movies, hairstyles, clothes, shoes, and swimwear.

Meanwhile, our PTA announced mini-grants to teachers for classroom supplies, so I was able to purchase new children's books on sexism and gender. When I shared the new books with the girls, they pored over them excitedly.

"Oh, look at this book! It's all about a woman astronaut."

"*Jacob's New Dress*, that is so cool!"

"This book is about girl inventors. Did you know a woman invented windshield wipers?" We talked about ways to incorporate the books into our project and decided that after the Three Circles Activity, students would choose a book to read and create a poster that addressed that book's main message.

A few days later, I ran into Allie's mom at school. She commented on how happy Allie was being in Peace Club and how excited she was to work on our gender unit. Her words meant a lot. I also checked in with Alexis's mom several times. As we planned the unit, I asked myself more than once if discussing a child's experiences with gender so openly with her classmates was overstepping my bounds. I wondered if this was something that parents would prefer to do on their own. But Alexis's mom reassured me that the unit we were creating had her blessing and, in fact, was appreciated.

"I Want to Shout Out My Feelings"

As we worked on the unit, the girls deepened their relationship and shared more of their experiences. "One time my family was eating at a Mexican restaurant," Alexis said. "The waiter kept referring to me as '*el niño*' and I had to keep saying, '*¡Soy una niña! ¡Soy una niña!*' But the waiter just didn't seem to really believe me."

"What do you say when someone treats you unkindly?" I asked. Allie explained that she often felt a lot of pressure to be kind, and that it was sometimes hard. "If someone bullies me, it's on purpose and so it's hard to be kind back. But if someone's just wondering if I'm a girl or a boy, it's easier to be nice because they're curious and don't know."

Alexis added, "Sometimes I want to shout out my feelings at the top of my lungs and tell people how I really feel."

"And what would you shout out?" I asked.

"I'm a girl! I'm a girl! Believe me when I tell you—I'm a girl!"

"Yeah, it's like people not accepting that we're the experts on who we are."

The next time we met, I began by asking if there was anything about our previous conversations that they wanted to discuss.

"I was thinking that the worst kind of bullying is not being able to use the bathroom because of the sign," Allie said.

"Say more about that," I suggested.

"Well, when we go to the bathroom, sometimes we're in lines— like a boy line and a girl line. And sometimes when I get into the girl line, people say, 'No—you're supposed to be in the boy line.'"

In a quiet voice, Alexis added: "That happens to me, too. One time when I was taking a theater class, we had a bathroom break. A girl told the teachers: 'A boy went in the girls' bathroom! A boy went in the girls' bathroom! A boy went in the girls' bathroom!' I told her, 'I'm not a boy, I'm a girl.' But she kept arguing with me. The other kids know if I'm a boy or a girl. They just don't accept it."

I asked if there was anything else they would like to add before moving into the planning portion of our meeting. Alexis looked at Allie with sheer joy and said, "I am so glad I know you, Allie! It's like finally I feel someone really understands me!"

"Thanks," said Allie. "I was thinking the same thing."

We began to plan out the following day's lesson. I began by asking: "How would you explain to your classmates what this project is about? For example, a unit on . . ."

"I think I would say we are doing a unit about gender problems," said Allie.

"Gender problems," I echoed.

"No!" responded both girls.

"So what is it you want? You want gender . . ."

"Acceptance," Alexis said. Allie agreed.

I agreed as well. "I find it's often more powerful to say what we want instead of what we are against."

We created an agenda for the following day's project, I typed it up and made copies, and we were ready to go.

Alexis and Allie Lead the Class

The following day, my students gathered together in a circle on the classroom rug and Alexis started things off by introducing herself. After Allie did the same, Alexis explained that she and Allie often get bullied because of the clothes they choose to wear. "Lots of times we don't feel accepted for who we are," added Allie.

Alexis continued: "And so we are doing a project about gender acceptance and trying to let people know and understand that we are girls—no matter how we dress."

"What do you think gender is?" Allie asked the students.

Emma immediately responded, "If you are a boy or a girl."

Allie confidently explained: "Gender could be a lot of possibilities. Like if someone is born a girl or a boy, and they felt that was the way they were supposed to be in their life. But gender could also be someone who is born a boy who felt like they were a girl, or someone who is born a girl and wished they were a boy."

"Or maybe," I added, "someone feels like they're in the middle—they don't want to have to choose boy or girl. Whatever someone feels inside themselves, that's okay.

"Even if you feel like a girl and everyone knows you're a girl, you still might want to do things that some people think are boy things—like Power Rangers. Or you might be a boy and want to play with dolls or wear jewelry. So lots of people don't always want to have to choose between boy and girl when there are unfair rules about gender."

Alexis asked if there were any questions and then Allie explained the Three Circles Activity. Alexis described the twelve categories and gave everyone a copy of them, along with some sticky notes. I re-iterated the instructions: "Let's start with the category Sports. Ask yourself: 'Can I think of a sport that only a girl would like—or a sport that only a boy would like—or a sport that both boys and girls might like?' Write the name of that sport on a sticky note and put it on the appropriate circle. Don't worry about spelling. Take your time to think before writing." Then I instructed the students to work their way through the other eleven categories.

The room bustled for twenty minutes as the students explored ideas, wrote them down, and stuck them onto one of the large circles. Alexis and Allie then took turns reading through many of the sticky notes, and then asked, "Were there some ideas you had an opinion about?" The room was alive with comments, questions, agreements, disagreements, and lots of thinking!

We Practice Peacemaking

As we talked about responses to the Clothes category, I asked: "Why do you think some people bullied Alexis and Allie for the kinds of T-shirts and pants they wore?"

Katie commented: "Maybe someone bullies someone else because they're thinking, 'You're not like me. If you're different from me, then you're not wearing the right kinds of clothes. So I'll bully you.' And, like Alexis said in the beginning, people keep asking if she's a boy or a girl. When they're not sure, they just bully her."

Emma slowly raised her hand. "I've been thinking about some-thing. I've seen people stare at Alexis because they think she's a boy. And they make gross faces because they think she is a boy going into the girls' bathroom."

"Did you say anything to them?" I asked.

"One time I did. I said, 'Excuse me, she's a girl, so she does have a right to go in the girls' bathroom. So leave her alone.' And then they actually stopped bothering her. But the year before, I didn't say any-thing because I really didn't know if Alexis was a girl or a boy."

I explained that what Emma did was important because she was trying to interrupt the bullying behavior that was taking place. I added that if you see bullying and don't say anything, it's like sending the message that it is okay to treat people that way. "What you might do is say something to interrupt the bullying, or if that doesn't solve the problem, go ask an adult to help you. Who wants to act the problem out, along with a way to try to solve it?"

Many hands went up. Alexis wanted to play herself and Emma played the person who wouldn't believe Alexis. Katie interrupted the bullying by saying, "Excuse me, but she told you she is a girl. You should just believe her."

Reuben blurted out, "And you should believe her the first time!" followed by applause from several of the students.

I asked: "How many of you have heard someone asking if a student was a boy or a girl, not believing the answer they received, so they kept asking the question over and over again?"

All the students' hands went up. "And how many of you think you know what you might say if you overheard that type of thing again?"

All the students' hands went up again.

"And what you are doing is called?"

"Interrupt bullying!"

"Have any of you heard a boy being made fun of in a similar way?" No one had. "But is that something you could interrupt in the same kind of way?"

"Yes!"

"Think about the many ways we've tried to help each other within our classroom learn to make better choices about how we treat each other. A really important part of peacemaking is helping other people make better choices, and it takes a lot of courage to do that. Anything else anyone wants to say?"

The room was quiet for a moment and then a few students spoke.

"I feel sorry for you, Alexis and Allie, that you got bullied just for being yourselves."

"I am sorry for how people treated you. And I am glad you are my friends."

Diego was the last to speak. "I am sorry I didn't believe you were a girl the first time you told me that. I will always believe you now."

In the weeks that followed, students chose one of our new picture books. Most students worked in pairs, a few preferred to work alone. After reading their books and figuring out the central message, students created posters. Although the original plan was to take a proactive stance against bullying by displaying the posters in our schools' hallways at the start of the next school year, instead the posters were included in a multimedia exhibit on androgyny by a local photographer.

Doing any classroom project for the first time always has an element of the unknown. I especially did not know how this unit would turn out with students sharing the helm for the project's development and implementation. What guided me more than anything was knowing that this unit evolved from the lives of two of my students and the incessant bullying they had experienced. It was their story that needed to be told, their experiences that needed to be understood, and their voices that needed to be heard.

Along the way, I learned how important it is to not put children in a "binary box." The traditional gender binary system is one that requires everyone to identify and be raised as either a boy or a girl— based on the sex one is assigned at birth. This rigidity forces some children to live out an identity that is not their own. And rigid gender stereotypes limit all of us in our thinking, creativity, and life choices. Children need time and freedom to explore their own gender identification and to know that the choices they make do not have to be static.

At the unit's completion I asked Alexis what these past few weeks meant to her. "I think everybody now accepts me for who I am." Raising both arms high in the air, she grinned and loudly exclaimed, "Finally!"

Nothing About Us,
Without Us, Is for Us

Hazel Edwards and Maya Lindberg in conversation

Hazel Edwards is a proud Philadelphia trans-community advocate and youth leader. She conducts research and analyzes data to improve the school climate for transgender and gender-nonconforming students in the Philadelphia school district.

Maya Lindberg is a writer and associate editor for Teaching Tolerance. *She previously worked as a writer for the Choices Program at Brown University.*

Meet Hazel Edwards, a passionate advocate and youth leader for Philadelphia's trans community. At just eighteen years old, she co-authored a policy for the School District of Philadelphia that established protections for transgender and gender-nonconforming students. Now twenty, she serves as an educator and outreach specialist with the Attic Youth Center, the only independent LGBTQ youth center in Philadelphia.

Edwards recently earned her GED and is focused on starting her undergraduate studies; she eventually plans to pursue a career in social work and art therapy for trans youth. She spoke with *Teaching Tolerance* in 2017 about her school experiences, her activism, and how educators can be the advocates trans students need.

M.L.: *How did you become an advocate and youth leader for Philadelphia's trans community?*

H.E.: I started doing my activism work when I was pushed out of my single-sex school in Philadelphia. My principal wanted to have a conversation about my absences and tardies, and I realized in the middle of the conversation that I was not able to explain myself without telling him that I'm trans and not feeling comfortable at this school was a result.

He had no idea what I was talking about when I was trying to explain my gender identity to him, so he brought in the guidance counselor. The guidance counselor was telling me that I couldn't get my hair done, my nails done or wear makeup, even though none of these things were against the rules. I just wanted to be able to express my gender, but I had no problem with the uniform.

[M]y guidance counselor said, "You are a boy," and at that moment, I felt like she was using her own internal bias to dictate the ways that she did her job. I felt invalidated. I felt like there's no point [in] finishing this conversation, so that's why I packed up my stuff and never went back to that school as a student.

Then I found an internship on social media at the Attic Youth Center called the Justice League. It's an internship for LGBTQ youth of color to talk about their experiences in systems of oppression and also educate youth and adults on different intersecting systems of oppression.

That's what made me a youth leader in the trans community.

Over time, within doing the work at the Attic, my old school actually requested a sensitivity training. I was one of the co-facilitators doing the gender and sexuality training for eighty-six of my old faculty members. After the workshop, my old principal came up to me and said, "The student is now the teacher," with tears in his eyes. That was also one of the most empowering moments for me, where I knew I had a gift of being able to share my story and to inspire folks.

Intersectionality

I read the following quote by you: "Nothing about us, without us, is for us." What meaning does it hold for you?

If youth, and specifically trans youth, are not given seats at the table to be able to bring their perspectives and their experiences and the ways that they could be best supported, then the policy or the legislation or whatever the rule is will not adequately support [them].

Cisgender folks don't know all of the necessary needs of trans folks. "Cisgender," C-I-S, meaning "same" in Latin, means your gender identity and assigned sex align. And predominantly cis and straight folks are the ones making the policies and making the legislation about trans people and about LGB people.

The resources and the best practices when working with trans youth are different from working with LGB youth, and that's important to recognize as well. Trans is a gender identity that is thrown into an acronym full of sexual identities that often get conflated, which is why service providers aren't always adequately equipped with best practices when working with trans folks.

You co-authored the School District of Philadelphia's Policy 252 that put in protections for transgender and gender-nonconforming youth. How did this policy come about?
A University of Pennsylvania professor wanted to get protections for her trans daughter, so she came to the Attic Youth Center. I shared my experience, as [did] three other young folks at the Attic. All of us sat in a meeting with some folks from the Philadelphia school district and with the parent. The school district heard our stories and said that something needs to be done, but that's a thing that we've always heard and nothing ever came out of it. So the parent, the professor at Penn, came to Justice League meetings and we looked at model policies. A lot of the model policies out there don't talk about gender-nonconforming identities or nonbinary identities, or give many protections to those trans folks.

One of the things that we saw was a lot of language of "consistent and persistent." "If this young person is coming in consistently and persistently in the expression of their gender that aligns with their gender identity, then that young person's gender identity will then be confirmed." I never felt comfortable even walking through my neighborhood or going other places consistently and persistently in my gender identity as I am now. Also, for many young folks at the Attic

Youth Center, they come in with one set of clothes, usually a school uniform, and then change their clothes for about one to two hours that they're going to be at the Attic and then change back into their clothes that they came in with to leave. Maybe because that young person may not have accepting family. Maybe that young person doesn't feel safe in their neighborhood.

After a few other folks and I crafted the policy, the professor sent it out to the district and it almost immediately was unanimously passed. I saw it on the news one day when I was walking home, and I was extremely happy and ecstatic. If a young person comes out to you, [under] this policy the administration has to support them. The administration has to honor their identity and their pronouns and their names, which is very powerful. I wish it was a policy that I could [have] use[d] for myself when I was in school.

And the only thing that the Philadelphia school district added is that every staff member has to be trained on gender identity. That's what brought me into helping with training for thousands of faculty members in the Philadelphia school district. I, [along with about twenty other trainers], did the training specifically on gender identity, gender expression, and assigned sex.

How can educators create trans-inclusive classrooms and schools?
Throw some trans history in there. Throw some queer history into your classes—in positive ways. In history class, you could talk a little bit about Stonewall while talking about civil rights movements. You could also [explain] that Stonewall was started by Marsha P. Johnson, a black trans woman who threw a shot glass and a brick that initiated the Stonewall Riots, which is the reason why we have gay pride.[1]

If LGBTQ youth don't see themselves represented in the curriculum that they're being given, they could totally zone out of it and disengage from education altogether.

[Celebrate] Day of Silence for those youth who don't have voices or that are not confident or comfortable enough with having their voice out there.[2]

Intervene, step in—if [you] hear homophobic or transphobic comments—with adequate disciplinary action, instead of just throwing it under the rug, which is what I hear from a lot of interviewees when I interview trans youth for the School of Social Policy and Practice at the University of Pennsylvania. That is one of the main things that I see: lack of advocacy from cisgender allies for the trans community.

Is there anything you would like to add that we haven't talked about?
When I came out as trans and I was pushed out of my school, shortly after, I was pushed out of my home as well. Me and my mom had a lot of issues and conflicts, and within those issues and conflicts, she would bring up my gender and say transphobic remarks to me that I wasn't accepting lightly.

That ultimately resulted in me not feeling safe or comfortable in the household anymore, so I was basically given an invitation to leave and I took it. I've experienced time being street homeless, couch surfing, and sometimes my mom would let me come in and then something would happen and I would leave again. Probably for about a year or so, I would say I was bouncing back and forth. I would identify myself as being homeless because I was unstably housed and supporting myself.

But because of the work and the advocacy I'm doing, I'm now able to financially support myself, which is a blessing. I wouldn't have known that half of Philadelphia would know who I am in the LGBTQ community. I didn't know that I would win a National Youth Leadership award [from the National LGBTQ Task Force]. All of these things just kind of happened, and all I was doing was the work that I'm passionate about.

Notes

1. Dalvin Brown, "Marsha P. Johnson: Transgender Hero of Stonewall Riots Finally Gets Her Due," *USA Today*, March 27, 2019, https://www.usatoday.com/story/news/investigations/2019/03/27/black-history-marsha-johnson-and-stonewall-riots/2353538002.

2. The Gay, Lesbian and Straight Education Network, GLSEN (referred to as "glisten"), founded a Day of Silence. It's a student-led national event where folks take a vow of silence to highlight the silencing and erasure of LGBTQ people at school. https://www.glsen.org/day-silence.

Climate
Matters

Climate Science Meets a Stubborn Obstacle: Students

Amy Harmon

Amy Harmon is a national correspondent for the New York Times, *covering the intersection of science and society. She has won two Pulitzer Prizes, one for her series "The DNA Age" and another as part of a team for the series "How Race Is Lived in America." She has received a Guggenheim Fellowship in science writing and is the author of the short story "Asperger Love."*

To Gwen Beatty, a junior at the high school in this proud, struggling, Trump-supporting town, the new science teacher's lessons on climate change seemed explicitly designed to provoke her.

So she provoked him back.

When the teacher, James Sutter, ascribed the recent warming of the Earth to heat-trapping gases released by burning fossil fuels like the coal her father had once mined, she asserted that it could be a result of other, natural causes.

When he described the flooding, droughts, and fierce storms that scientists predict within the century if such carbon emissions are not sharply reduced, she challenged him to prove it.

"Scientists are wrong all the time," she said with a shrug, echoing those celebrating President Trump's announcement that the United States would withdraw from the Paris climate accord.

When Mr. Sutter lamented that information about climate change had been removed from the White House website after Mr. Trump's inauguration, she rolled her eyes.

"It's *his* website," she said.

For his part, Mr. Sutter occasionally fell short of his goal of providing Gwen—the most vocal of a raft of student climate skeptics—with calm, evidence-based responses. "Why would I lie to you?" he demanded one morning. "It's not like I'm making a lot of money here."

She was, he knew, a straight-A student. She would have had no trouble comprehending the evidence, embedded in ancient tree rings, ice, leaves, and shells, as well as sophisticated computer models, that atmospheric carbon dioxide is the chief culprit when it comes to warming the world. Or the graph he showed of how sharply it has spiked since the industrial revolution, when humans began pumping vast quantities of it into the air.

Thinking it a useful soothing device, Mr. Sutter assented to Gwen's request that she be allowed to sand the bark off the sections of wood he used to illustrate tree rings during class. When she did so with an energy that, classmates said, increased during discussion points with which she disagreed, he let it go.

When she insisted that teachers "are supposed to be open to opinions," however, Mr. Sutter held his ground.

"It's not about opinions," he told her. "It's about the evidence."

"It's like you can't disagree with a scientist or you're 'denying science,'" she sniffed to her friends.

Gwen, seventeen, could not put her finger on why she found Mr. Sutter, whose biology class she had enjoyed, suddenly so insufferable. Mr. Sutter, sensing that his facts and figures were not helping, was at a loss. And the day she grew so agitated by a documentary he was showing that she bolted out of the school left them both shaken.

"I have a runner," Mr. Sutter called down to the office, switching off the video.

He had chosen the video, an episode from an Emmy Award–winning series that featured a Christian climate activist and high production values as a counterpoint to another of Gwen's objections, that a belief in climate change does not jibe with Christianity.

"It was just so biased toward saying climate change is real," she said later, trying to explain her flight. "And that all these people that I pretty much am like are wrong and stupid."

Classroom Culture Wars

As more of the nation's teachers seek to integrate climate science into the curriculum, many of them are reckoning with students for whom suspicion of the subject is deeply rooted. In rural Wellston, Ohio, a former coal and manufacturing town seeking its next act, rejecting the key findings of climate science can seem like a matter of loyalty to a way of life already under siege. Originally tied, perhaps, to economic self-interest, climate skepticism has itself become a proxy for conservative ideals of hard work, small government, and what people here call "self-sustainability."

Assiduously promoted by fossil fuel interests, that powerful link to a collective worldview largely explains why just 22 percent of Mr. Trump's supporters in a 2016 poll said they believed that human activity is warming the planet, compared with half of all registered voters. And the prevailing outlook among his base may in turn have facilitated the president's move to withdraw from the global agreement to battle rising temperatures.

"What people 'believe' about global warming doesn't reflect what they know," Dan Kahan, a Yale researcher who studies political polarization, has stressed in talks, papers, and blog posts. "It expresses who they are."

But public-school science classrooms are also proving to be a rare place where views on climate change may shift, research has found. There, in contrast with much of adult life, it can be hard to entirely tune out new information.

"Adolescents are still heavily influenced by their parents, but they're also figuring themselves out," said Kathryn Stevenson, a researcher at North Carolina State University who studies climate literacy.

Gwen's father died when she was young, and her mother and uncle, both Trump supporters, doubt climate change as much as she does.

"If she was in math class and the teacher told her two plus two equals four and she argued with him about that, I would say she's wrong," said her uncle, Mark Beatty. "But no one knows if she's wrong."

As Gwen clashed with her teacher over the notion of human-caused climate change, one of her best friends, Jacynda Patton, was still circling the taboo subject. "I learned some stuff, that's all," Jacynda told Gwen, on whom she often relied to supply the $2.40 for school lunch that she could not otherwise afford.

Hired a year earlier, Mr. Sutter was the first science teacher at Wellston to emphasize climate science. He happened to do so at a time when the mounting evidence of the toll that global warming is likely to take, and the Trump administration's considerable efforts to discredit those findings, are drawing new attention to the classroom from both sides of the nation's culture war.

Since March, the Heartland Institute, a think tank that rejects the scientific consensus on climate change, has sent tens of thousands of science teachers a book of misinformation titled "Why Scientists Disagree About Global Warming," in an effort to influence "the next generation of thought," said Joseph Bast, the group's chief executive.

The Alliance for Climate Education, which runs assemblies based on the consensus science for high schools across the country, received new funding from a donor who sees teenagers as the best means of reaching and influencing their parents.

Idaho, however, this year joined several other states that have declined to adopt new science standards that emphasize the role human activities play in climate change.

At Wellston, where most students live below the poverty line and the needle-strewn bike path that abuts the marching band's practice field is known as "heroin highway," climate change is not regarded as the most pressing issue. And since most Wellston graduates typically do not go on to obtain a four-year college degree, this may be the only chance many of them have to study the impact of global warming.

But Mr. Sutter's classroom shows how curriculum can sometimes influence culture on a subject that stands to have a more profound impact on today's high schoolers than their parents.

"I thought it would be an easy A," said Jacynda, sixteen, an outspoken Trump supporter. "It wasn't."

God's Gift to Wellston?

Mr. Sutter, who grew up three hours north of Wellston in the largely Democratic city of Akron, applied for the job at Wellston High straight from a program to recruit science professionals into teaching, a kind of science-focused Teach for America.

He already had a graduate-level certificate in environmental science from the University of Akron and a private sector job assessing environmental risk for corporations. But a series of personal crises that included his sister's suicide, he said, had compelled him to look for a way to channel his knowledge to more meaningful use.

The fellowship gave him a degree in science education in exchange for a three-year commitment to teach in a high-needs Ohio school district. Megan Sowers, the principal, had been looking for someone qualified to teach an Advanced Placement course, which could help improve her financially challenged school's poor performance ranking. She hired him on the spot.

But at a school where most teachers were raised in the same southeastern corner of Appalachian Ohio as their students, Mr. Sutter's credentials themselves could raise hackles.

"He says, 'I left a higher-paying job to come teach in an area like this,'" Jacynda recalled.

"We're like, 'What is that supposed to mean?'"

"He acts," Gwen said with her patented eye roll, "like he's God's gift to Wellston."

In truth, he was largely winging it.

Some twenty states, including a handful of red ones, have recently begun requiring students to learn that human activity is a major cause of climate change, but few, if any, have provided a road map for how to teach it, and most science teachers, according to one recent survey, spend at most two hours on the subject.

Chagrined to learn that none of his students could recall a school visit by a scientist, Mr. Sutter hosted several graduate students from nearby Ohio University.

On a field trip to a biology laboratory there, many of his students took their first ride on an escalator. To illustrate why some scientists in the 1970s believed the world was cooling rather than warming ("So why should we believe them now?" students sometimes asked), he brought in a 1968 push-button phone and a 1980s Nintendo game cartridge.

"Our data and our ability to process it is just so much better now," he said.

In the AP class, Mr. Sutter took an informal poll midway through: in all, fourteen of seventeen students said their parents thought he was, at best, wasting their time. "My stepdad says they're brainwashing me," one said.

Jacynda's father, for one, did not raise an eyebrow when his daughter stopped attending Mr. Sutter's class for a period in the early winter. A former coal miner who had endured two years of unemployment before taking a construction job, he declined a request to talk about it.

"I think it's that it's taken a lot from him," Jacynda said. "He sees it as the environmental people have taken his job."

And having listened to Mr. Sutter reiterate the overwhelming agreement among scientists regarding humanity's role in global warming in answer to another classmate's questions—"What if we're not the cause of it? What if this is something that's natural?"—Jacynda texted the classmate one night using an expletive to refer to Mr. Sutter's teaching approach.

But even the staunchest climate-change skeptics could not ignore the dearth of snow days last winter, the cap to a year that turned out to be the warmest Earth has experienced since 1880, according to NASA. The high mark eclipsed the record set just the year before, which had eclipsed the year before that.

In woods behind the school, where Mr. Sutter had his students scout out a nature trail, he showed them the preponderance of emerald ash borers, an invasive insect that, because of the warm weather, had not experienced the usual die-off that winter. There was flooding, too: once, more than five-and-a-half inches of rain fell in forty-eight hours.

The field trip to a local stream where the water runs neon orange also made an impression. Mr. Sutter had the class collect water samples: the pH levels were as acidic as "the white vinegar you buy at a grocery store," he told them. And the drainage, they could see, was from the mine.

It was the realization that she had failed to grasp the damage done to her immediate environment, Jacynda said, that made her begin to pay more attention. She did some reading. She also began thinking that she might enjoy a job working for the Environmental Protection Agency—until she learned that, under Mr. Trump, the agency would undergo huge layoffs.

"Okay, I'm not going to lie. I did a 180," she said that afternoon in the library with Gwen, casting a guilty look at her friend. "This is happening, and we have to fix it."

After fleeing Mr. Sutter's classroom that day, Gwen never returned, a pragmatic decision about which he has regrets. "That's one student I feel I failed a little bit," he said.

As an alternative, Gwen took an online class for environmental science credit, which she does not recall ever mentioning climate change. She and Jacynda had other things to talk about, like planning a bonfire after prom.

As they tried on dresses last month, Jacynda mentioned that others in their circle, including the boys they had invited to prom, believed the world was dangerously warming, and that humans were to blame. By the last days of school, most of Mr. Sutter's doubters, in fact, had come to that conclusion.

"I know," Gwen said, pausing for a moment. "Now help me zip this up."

Teachers vs. Climate Change: The Story of Teachers' Work for Climate Justice in Portland, Oregon

Bill Bigelow

Bill Bigelow taught high-school social studies for almost thirty years and is curriculum editor of Rethinking Schools *magazine and co-director of the Zinn Education Project. He is the author or co-editor of many Rethinking Schools publications, including* A People's History for the Classroom; The Line Between Us: Teaching About the Border and Mexican Immigration; Rethinking Globalization: Teaching for Justice in an Unjust World; Rethinking Our Classrooms, volumes 1 and 2; Rethinking Columbus: The Next 500 Years; *and* A People's Curriculum for the Earth: Teaching Climate Change and the Environmental Crisis.

PORTLAND, OREGON, WHERE I HAVE LIVED AND WORKED FOR MORE than forty years, has a reputation as a progressive and environmentally conscious city. So imagine teachers' surprise when we learned in 2007 that the school district had purchased a textbook, McDougal Littell's *Modern World History*, which relegated discussion of climate change to three miserable paragraphs buried on page 679. "Not all scientists agree with the theory of the greenhouse effect," it read, and went on to blame poor countries for dragging their heels on climate solutions while wealthy countries were leading the way.[1] The book failed to include a single quote from anyone touched by climate change. And this was the text to be used in modern world history classes, taken by almost all students in Portland high schools.

Social studies teachers in Portland have long been a feisty lot, and many simply ignored this district-adopted textbook or used it for target practice to engage students in "talkback" reading activities looking at whose perspectives the book ignored or distorted. But in the fall of 2015, teachers, parents, students, and climate justice activists began meeting to chart a different response to the failure of the school district to deal forthrightly with what is arguably the most serious crisis facing humanity. My colleague Tim Swinehart and I had worked for years to produce a comprehensive resource for teachers—a book of role plays, simulations, and student-friendly readings, *A People's Curriculum for the Earth: Teaching Climate Change and the Environmental Crisis* (Rethinking Schools), published earlier that year. 350PDX, the local affiliate of the global climate justice organization, 350.org, invited us to lead a workshop based on the book to involve educators and climate activists in exploring ways that we could work together to get the school district to take more affirmative action on the climate crisis.

Urged on by environmental justice activists, Portland's city council had recently passed a resolution banning new fossil fuel infrastructure in the city. In the glow of this bold move, the teachers and activists at the 350PDX workshop that Tim and I led hatched the idea of working on a climate justice resolution to bring to the school board. We wanted board members to commit the school district to abandon the use of textbooks that minimized the severity of the climate crisis or its social roots, and to take a more robust approach to climate justice professional development and curriculum sharing.

Teachers weren't the only ones demanding change. Students at one Portland high school, similarly disgusted by the *Modern World History* textbook, demanded a meeting with the assistant superintendent in charge of teaching and learning to express their grievances about this book, and to demand alternatives. They knew the book lots better than he did, and in their meeting, peppered him with example after indefensible example of passages that have no place in a public school classroom.

We began to collaborate. Our group of teachers, students, parents, and climate activists gave ourselves a name—Educating for Climate Justice—and over several months of evening meetings, we crafted a resolution to bring to the school board. The process of agreeing on language for the resolution was time-consuming but exhilarating. It was one thing to know that we wanted the school district to scrap wretched textbooks like *Modern World History*, but more difficult to articulate precisely what we wanted instead.

We were startled by how many people assumed that we were drafting a resolution aimed simply at greater inclusion of "climate literacy" in science classes. No doubt, that was one aspect of our work. But committee members saw this as a *social* issue, not strictly a scientific one. As Naomi Klein emphasized in the subtitle of her book *This Changes Everything*, the root of the crisis lies in how wealth and power are structured in our society; it's *capitalism versus the climate*. Thus in our resolution, we emphasized that "it is essential that in their classes and other school activities students probe the causes and consequences of the climate crisis . . ." and explore "potential solutions that address the root causes of the crisis."[2] This put justice at the heart of our work, not carbon dioxide.

We intended the resolution to acknowledge the effects of climate change as a local issue, that these effects are felt not only far away in the Arctic or sub-Saharan Africa. However, we wanted to balance the local with the global. Nothing is more central to the climate crisis than inequality. And it is inequality that is the common denominator, whether we are talking about climate impacts here in Portland next to the Columbia River, or half a world away in Bangladesh next to the Brahmaputra River. As the resolution indicated, a climate justice curriculum should seek to center the lives and experiences "of people from 'frontline' communities, which have been the first and hardest hit by climate change." For years, Portland Public Schools has focused on equity. Well, climate change is the mother of all equity issues, as the people least responsible for this planet-threatening crisis are the first to suffer, and the ones most responsible for causing it are the best positioned to insulate themselves from its worst effects.

Too often, when school districts decide on new curricular

initiatives, they operate from a consumer paradigm: commence the hunt for different programs or texts to purchase, and then impose these on teachers. Instead, we saw the school district's climate justice work as a grassroots, collective project of people throughout the school system: professional development and curriculum materials would be fashioned "in ways that are participatory, imaginative, and respectful of students' and teachers' creativity and eagerness to be part of addressing global problems, and that build a sense of personal efficacy and empowerment."

Last but not least, we insisted that student activism is the necessary response to the immense threat of the climate crisis: "All Portland Public Schools students should develop confidence and passion when it comes to making a positive difference in society, and come to see themselves as activists and leaders for social and environmental justice . . . ; and it is vital that students reflect on local impacts of the climate crisis, and recognize how their own communities and lives are implicated."

Our resolution was expansive and ambitious, but right-wing media throughout the country would focus their outrage on the resolution's final sentence: "[Portland Public Schools] will abandon the use of any adopted text material that is found to express doubt about the severity of the climate crisis or its root in human activities." More on that in a moment.

As Educating for Climate Justice closed in on a final draft, we began to reach out to community groups to enlist their endorsement, and ultimately signed on more than thirty organizations, including Oregon Physicians for Social Responsibility, the Sierra Club, the Portland Association of Teachers (the teachers union), Climate Jobs PDX, Rising Tide, the Climate Action Coalition, the Raging Grannies, several synagogues, and of course, 350PDX.[3]

In May 2016, members of our committee and community supporters—many of us dressed in Portland's climate justice red—gathered for a short but spirited rally at the high school where the school board was meeting. Prior to our testimony in support of our resolution, we were introduced by board member Mike Rosen, who had supported our work from the beginning and was our liaison with the school board. Six of us testified before the school board, including Gabrielle Lemieux, a student who had helped craft our resolution from the very beginning. The week before the board meeting, many in our committee had traveled to a "Keep It in the Ground" demonstration in Anacortes, Washington, home to two oil refineries. Part of the demonstration was a blockade of railroad tracks into the oil refineries. Gaby testified:

> People said to me, "You have a whole lifetime ahead of you to get arrested, to do this kind of work."
> My response is: We don't have my lifetime to wait. We don't even have the couple years it will be before I'm truly an adult. My action starts now, or it works never. Your action, this action, accepting this resolution and taking on the responsibility as educators to create an effective, engaging, and comprehensive climate curriculum, that starts now. It *must* start now.

The school board, a seven-member body elected citywide, voted unanimously to support our resolution.

Our post-resolution glee was short lived. The next day, a headline in the *Portland Tribune* shouted, "Portland School Board Bans Climate-Change Denying Materials." The school board's resolution never mentioned the word "ban," but we should have been prepared for what the *L.A. Times* called the "firestorm" of right-wing media vitriol that ensued. The *Tribune* article generated 3,152 online comments, calling us "latter day inquisitors" and worse, and drew the attention of Fox News, the *Washington Times*, the *National Review*, Glenn Beck's *The Blaze*, the Heartland Institute, and others. All joined the chorus to denounce censorship and book banning, with some outlets painting us as book burners. An *Accuracy in Media* article, "The Red Guards Are Green," quoted Patrick Wood, editor of *Technocracy News & Trends*: "Will they ban materials from the homes of students? What will be the punishment for being caught with such materials on Portland Public School campuses?" Portland's most widely read newspaper, the *Oregonian*, accused us of "indoctrination."

But there were also welcome gestures of solidarity, like the organization Climate Parents, which collected more than a thousand signatures thanking Portland's school board for passing the resolution.[4]

The storm of controversy caught us off-guard and for a few weeks distracted us from the work of beginning to implement the resolution. But over the summer, as "banning" accusations waned, we met with school district officials and established ourselves as a formal school district committee, the Portland Public Schools Climate Justice Committee.

Frontline Communities

Our committee never made a conscious decision to postpone our evaluation of Portland textbooks, but given the storm of controversy, we decided to let those winds die down and return to the problem of biased textbooks later in the year.

Pushing the school district to take climate justice seriously meant that we could not just proceed sequentially.

We were fortunate that our committee launched just as the Marshall Islands performance poet Kathy Jetñil-Kijiner arrived in Portland to live here part of the year. Kathy's poem, "Dear Matafele Peinam"—written to her seven-month-old daughter to open the 2014 United Nations climate talks in New York—had begun to work its way into the curriculum of some Portland teachers, and her work exemplified our commitment to center the lives and voices of people from frontline communities in our curriculum work. The poem, which Kathy performs from memory, "poetry slam" style, captures the existential threat of the climate crisis:

> *dear matafele peinam,*
>
> *i want to tell you about that lagoon*
> *that lucid, sleepy lagoon lounging against the sunrise*
> *men say that one day*
> *that lagoon will devour you*

they say it will gnaw at the shoreline
chew at the roots of your breadfruit trees
gulp down rows of your seawalls
and crunch your island's shattered bones

they say you, your daughter
and your granddaughter, too
will wander rootless
with only a passport to call home

But moves toward hope:

still
there are those who see us

hands reaching out
fists raising up
banners unfurling
megaphones booming
and we are
canoes blocking coal ships
we are
the radiance of solar villages
we are
the rich clean soil of the farmer's past
we are
petitions blooming from teenage fingertips
we are
families biking, recycling, reusing,
engineers dreaming, designing, building,
artists painting, dancing, writing
and we are spreading the word . . .

The Marshalls, located about halfway between Hawaii and Austra-
lia rise no higher than six feet above sea level. As Kathy offers simply
in her poem, "Tell Them": "We only have one road."

We contracted with Kathy for professional development with teachers, and sessions in Portland middle and high schools. Performance poetry is well suited to describe and denounce climate change. It is personal, story-rich, angry, accessible. Kathy's poetry is a cri de coeur that offers a glimpse into the enormity of a crisis that is drowning homes and cultures. And, as we would soon see, it is a form of creative expression that invites students to share their own lives, and to name the hurt and injustice closer to home about gentrification, police violence, proposed liquefied-natural-gas pipelines, and more.

We soon recognized that if we were serious about honoring the resolution's call to center the voices of people from frontline communities, those voices didn't focus only on climate change. In Kathy's work, the climate crisis was embedded in a historic web of colonial domination—the Marshalls were colonized first by the Germans, then Japanese, then Americans—and were literally ground zero for a decade of nuclear tests in the 1940s and 1950s that vaporized entire islands, and especially victimized women through radioactive pollution.

Starting in the fall of 2016, Kathy has led three professional development sessions for a couple hundred Portland educators, and thirty-three workshops for about two thousand students from six high schools and two middle schools. Some of these have been exclusively for Pacific Islander students, arguably one of the least-served student populations in our school district. These focused on climate issues, but also on racism, linguistic discrimination, and PI students' struggles to make a home in an overwhelmingly white city, with a legacy of racism hammered into its foundation. But these sessions with students from Fiji, Chuuk, Palau, American Samoa, Hawaii, the Ryuku Islands, Western Samoa, and Tonga were also joyful occasions of people finding community in institutions that at times make Pacific Islanders feel invisible. These workshops highlighted the intersection between climate justice education and ethnic studies: When the students gather, they articulate not only concerns about climate change but also about the curricular silence about their cultures, and other indigenous issues. As one young woman shared, "The only time they talk about Hawaii is when they mention Pearl Harbor."

Choking back tears at a school board meeting, Roosevelt High School twelfth-grade student Siale Ita, whose family is from Tonga, spoke of how moving it was to work with Kathy Jetñil-Kijiner: "As a young Pacific Islander woman, I have never in classrooms—sorry, it just gets me so emotional. I have never learned about climate change in any of my classrooms—science, history, and the effects it has on the Pacific Islands. My people are having to evacuate their homes."

Siale performed a poem in front of the school board inspired by Kathy's work that tracks the climate-changed ocean, inching higher on her island:

The water rising to her ankles,
She remembers those nights waking up to her home flooded yet again,
Learning there is nowhere on this island to escape the floods
The next morning she makes her daily offerings
into the ocean, whispering,
"Are you a friend or a foe?
Please spare us some more time.
I'll climb to the highest peak with my people on my back
if that is what it takes to find peace."

As Siale's poem progresses, the water rises to the woman's knees, her hips, her breasts, her shoulders, and finally to her head:

She is ready to surrender unto the sea.
Yet she hears the chants of her people from afar, screaming,
"We will not go, we will stay.
We will plant our feet into the earth."
She too will plant her feet into the earth.
She is staying on this island.

Professional Development

I began teaching in Portland in 1978. One of the persistent struggles that teachers face has focused on the question: who owns the curriculum? In the 1990s, Portland hired a new superintendent who was fond of telling people that nothing had been done in the way of curriculum in Portland. She was referring to the fact that Portland did not have a standardized curriculum with common assessments, instituted and closely monitored from the top. So even though Portland was home to a rich culture of curriculum development—quarterly teachers-teaching-teachers curriculum days; the Oregon Writing Project, one of the most vital sites in the National Writing Project network; and years of grassroots curriculum writing and sharing—to many administrators, all this added up to a big nothing.

As for the PPS Climate Justice Committee, we were concerned that once passed, our school board resolution might be buried in a central office file cabinet. But another concern was that the district would contract with an outfit to "deliver" professional development to teachers. As mentioned, the resolution proposes a very different curriculum development model, one that is "participatory" and "imaginative." One of our committee's first district-wide gatherings asked teachers to come together to imagine what climate justice looks like at their grade level and in their discipline. We were excited to have diverse teacher participants from early elementary, middle school Spanish, high school science, and lots in between.

In our first gathering, Rachel Hanes, a second-grade teacher and committee member, pointed out that the environmental standard at her grade level called for children to learn that plants need water and sunlight to grow. The prescribed experiment is to grow a sunflower and discuss how a sunflower might fare in different environments like a desert or the Arctic. There is nothing wrong with this sliver of knowledge, but as Rachel pointed out, this unambitious objective imagines that her students are much less capable than they are. She shared a profound "Storyline" curriculum she developed with colleagues at her school in which students construct a town and then are challenged to solve problems as a community. One of these is to respond to a proposal from the "Carson Environmental Oil Co." to "take part in an exciting new opportunity to create jobs and earn money for our city by allowing them to put a pipeline through the community. Although some trees will be cut down and some residents may need to be relocated, but they will be compensated!" The debates and learning that ensue are rich and intense, and Rachel shared with us her students' conversations about solidarity: What happens if our community rejects the pipeline and Carson decides to move it to a different community? As Rachel explained, "I want my students to see themselves not as hopeless victims in the struggle for climate justice but as actors who can have an impact on the world around them." Second graders.

As a career high-school social studies teacher, I was inspired to see what it looks like for second graders to take a critical look at the fossil fuel industry, and for third graders to represent people from around the world in a climate justice forum and express how they are affected by climate change. And as someone who almost flunked my own high school chemistry class, seeing how science can—and should—intersect seamlessly with social studies and other disciplines was a revelation. If only my own 1968 chemistry class had been so socially aware!

In subsequent meetings with some school district officials to discuss implementing the climate justice resolution in Portland schools, they have tried to figure out "where it goes" in the curriculum, as if there is a discrete "it" to be slotted into a particular discipline and grade level. Too often, climate change has been a curricular hot potato, with no one claiming it as theirs. However, as our teacher curriculum gatherings showed, climate justice work in schools "belongs" to all of us, and we can be inspired by one another's work.

Climate Warriors

In an audacious embrace of Portland's climate justice resolution, teachers in Madison High School's Citizen Chemistry for All course—a class enrolling more than three hundred sophomores in the school—adopted an essential question for the year: "Why are human changes to Earth's carbon cycles at the heart of climate destabilization?" Students would demonstrate their learning at a two-day Climate Justice Fair in Madison's library, in which they would represent "communities which are engaging as 'climate warriors,' providing critical analysis of their work and or proposing additional needed activism."

An honest, rigorous look at the science of climate change can be terrifying and disheartening. Falling into cynicism is a hazard one confronts simply by living in our society, with its inequality, violence, and lack of democracy. But add to that, knowledge of the inexorable rise of greenhouse gases in our atmosphere—and what this heat-trapping pollution means for the Earth—and despair feels like more than a threat, it feels like common sense. Knowing this, Madison teachers focused not purely on the science of climate destabilization, but also on the people who are taking action to reverse it, inviting students to research "Climate Warriors," those who have not given up, those who "know the truth," and yet are not defeated by it.

For the project, students had three areas of work they had to complete: Direct Action, Climate Justice Warrior Storytelling, and Listening and Reflecting at the Climate Fair. Direct actions could include simply writing a letter, designing a poster, or taking a stand in some way, but could also include making a short film, participating in a rally or hearing, or making a personal or family lifestyle change that could contribute to mitigating climate destabilization. Madison chemistry teachers—which included Treothe Bullock and Rachel Stagner, members of our PPS Climate Justice Committee, and Tim Kniser—required students to identify one of the climate-related crises or issues explored in class and to create a slideshow, poster, short film, podcast, or some other way to "show how a 'climate warrior' is fighting against this issue." And at the fair, students were expected to offer feedback to at least four other presenters.

I attended the first day of the fair. The library buzzed with anticipation. Treothe Bullock launched the day with the invitation: "There isn't anyone who has the answer. We're figuring it out." Every student received a "Climate Justice Passport" to take notes in. Students had to identify the climate warrior, the issue they are involved in, the chemistry connection, and to evaluate the proposed solution.

Students' "warriors" were diverse and included Xiuhtexcatl Martinez, a plaintiff in the landmark Our Children's Trust lawsuit, *Juliana v. United States of America*; Nobel Peace Prize–winner and former president of Ireland Mary Robinson, who works especially on the intersection of climate change and women's issues; Rose High Bear (Deg Hit'an Dine), producer of the NPR series *Wisdom of the Elders*; West Virginia mountaintop-removal activist Maria Gunnoe; Crystal Lameman, of Canada's Beaver Lake Cree Nation, featured in the film *This Changes Everything*; and Zack Rago, a reef aquarist and scuba diver who appears in the film *Chasing Coral*. The young woman presenting Rago as her "climate warrior" taught me more about coral during her short presentation than I'd ever known. (Did you know that coral is simultaneously rock, plant, and animal?)

Other students chose organizations or movements as their warriors rather than individuals. One student focused on 350.org, especially their "Keep It in the Ground" campaign—"They really want you and me to get involved in this." A couple students presented the indigenous movement to oppose the Dakota Access Pipeline (DAPL). About the pipeline's builders, Energy Transfer Partners, one student presenter commented: "There is not much depth to what they want. They just want more." And one student, clearly moved by her research, described her personal commitment to abandon eating meat because of cattle's out-sized carbon footprint.

Despair is always a step away when we begin looking deeply at the contours of our climate emergency. But in Madison's Climate Justice Warrior project students encountered the hope and determination of activists alongside the disturbing science of climate change. And as dire as the news can appear, our curriculum needn't be similarly grim. During the Climate Justice Fair, the Madison library was electric with laughter—students telling stories, others listening respectfully, blurting out the frequent "wow" and "I never knew that."

Textbooks: The Bad and the Ugly

In the testimony I gave to the school board in 2016 arguing for our climate justice resolution, I focused on two adopted textbooks, still currently in use, to highlight the need for alternative curriculum. I mentioned earlier the terrible *Modern World History*, but as egregious in its own way was a Pearson/Prentice Hall text, *Physical Science: Concepts in Action*, which finally gets around to mentioning climate change on page 782. The few paragraphs on the human source of a warming planet are soaked in doubt: "Human activities may also change climate over time. . . . One possible climate change is caused by the addition of carbon dioxide and certain other gases into the atmosphere." The text shrugs off the certainty of human-caused climate change with a timid vocabulary of "possible," "might," "could," and "may": "Carbon dioxide emissions from motor vehicles, power plants, and other sources may contribute to global warming"—a nothing-to-worry-about line that would be right at home in Koch brothers propaganda.[5]

So we knew that Portland schools used at least two problematic texts, but in spring 2017, our committee developed a rubric to evaluate *all* school district–adopted science and social studies textbooks— not just "environmental studies" texts—for their compliance with the school board's resolution. Criteria included:

- The text provides stories and examples that help students grasp the immediacy, systemic nature, and gravity of the climate crisis.
- The text includes actions that people are taking to address the climate crisis, locally and worldwide.
- The text emphasizes that all people are being affected by the climate crisis, but also highlights the inequitable effects of the crisis on certain groups (e.g., indigenous peoples, people in poverty, Pacific Islanders, people in sub-Saharan Africa, people dependent on glaciers for drinking water and irrigation, etc.).
- The text does not use conditional language that expresses doubt about the climate crisis (e.g., "Some scientists believe . . . ," "Human activities may change climate . . .").
- There are discussion and/or writing questions that provoke critical thinking.

Our committee invited individuals from our partner groups for a full-afternoon evaluation session and thirteen of us gathered at the school district administration building with fifteen adopted science

and social studies textbooks to assess whether all were as problematic as the ones we had previously critiqued. Our conclusion:
every adopted textbook was out of compliance with the school board's
resolution.

Not surprisingly, all the books ignored or dramatically minimized
the severity of the climate crisis. The high school economics textbook, *Contemporary Economics*, says nothing about climate change in
more than 700 pages. An adopted U.S. history text, *Pursuing American Ideals*, includes one sentence on climate change in 890 pages. The
high school text *Biology* includes three paragraphs in its 1,100 pages.
And on and on.

Reviewers also found lots of missed opportunities. The eighth-
grade adoption, *History Alive!: The United States Through Industrialization*, contains less than a paragraph relating to climate change in
505 pages. One PPS reviewer commented, "While this book goes
only through industrialization, the book fails to alert students to the
practices and ideology that will ultimately lead us to the climate crisis. These days a history text should do that." Another reviewer commented about Magruder's iconic *American Government*: "How can
a book about the U.S. government say nothing about the climate
crisis—or environmental policy more broadly? This is egregious, un-
acceptable." About the high school AP European history textbook
Western Civilizations, one reviewer noted that the book talks about the
pollution that came with the industrial revolution, but here, too, fails
to bring this up to the climate crisis. The book contains one sentence
on global warming out of its 1,063 pages. *American Spirit Reader*, an
AP/IB high school U.S. history adoption, includes nothing in its 538
pages relating to climate change. One reviewer noted, "As with other
books on U.S. history, there is an opportunity to look at early U.S.
history as the prologue to the climate crisis, but this book is utterly
silent."

To the extent that district-adopted textbooks discuss climate
change, no text suggests that students or ordinary people might play
a role in addressing this growing threat—or that "frontline communities" are themselves responding to the climate crisis. In its one
sentence on climate change, *History Alive!: Pursuing American Ideals*

says that "environmentalists fear" problems like global warming.[6] Indeed. But the climate justice resolution's intent is to underscore our students' *own* role in making the world a better place, rather than assigning concern and action only to scientists or environmentalists.

I suppose that none of this comes as a surprise. The giant corporations that produce these textbooks have no interest in students asking critical questions about the economic system that regards profit maximization as the highest aim. These corporations are themselves richly rewarded by a profit-first economy, so are unlikely to suggest that this economic system may be at the root of our environmental crisis. And, of course, multinational textbook publishers seek markets in states dominated by fossil fuel interests, and thus are reluctant to suggest that continuing to burn fossil fuels jeopardizes nature and humanity.

Nonetheless, our committee is preparing letters of "noncompliance" with the Portland Public Schools climate justice resolution to send to textbook publishers, cataloging how their textbooks fail to address climate issues in even mildly satisfactory ways. We are also sending letters to district middle school, science, and social studies teachers alerting them to our findings, and urging them to seek alternatives to these problematic resources.

Activists and Leaders

Here's the feature of the climate justice resolution that committee members probably invoke most often: "All Portland Public Schools students should develop confidence and passion when it comes to making a positive difference in society, and come to see themselves as activists and leaders for social and environmental justice." We especially want educators to know that it is the official policy of the school district that we should nurture students' activist sensibilities. And this is surely what our right-wing critics were most exercised about when they learned that the school board had passed this resolution—that school district leaders imagined schools as sites for activism.

There is no road map for how we can make sure that schools play a central role in addressing our climate emergency. Not only do commercially produced textbooks not have an answer to responding to the climate crisis, they are solidly part of the problem. The school board passed a magnificent resolution, but top administrators have offered tepid support for climate justice education and appear to remain attached to a model of teaching and learning that embraces "power standards" and programs developed at great distance from classrooms to be imposed on teachers.

At a recent cross-border teaching for social justice conference sponsored by the Surrey Teachers' Association and the British Columbia Teachers' Federation, keynote speaker Naomi Klein lamented that although our "leaders" occasionally pay lip service to the climate emergency, they act like everything is normal. Sadly, the same is true in our schools. At the level of school leadership, there is no sense of crisis, of urgency. This is the work that educators are called to.

In fact, we could have accomplished much of our climate justice work in Portland without an official school-board resolution. If there is something to be learned from our experience here it's that people of conscience need to find one another and begin to act. History teaches that anything good and decent and just we have in our society is because people organized to effect change. It's a lesson those of us connected to school communities need to take to heart. Our house is on fire. Let's act like it.

Notes

1. Roger B. Beck, et al., eds., *Modern World History: Patterns of Interaction* (McDougal Littell, 2007).

2. "Resolution No. 5272: Resolution to Develop an Implementation Plan for Climate Literacy," Portland Public Schools Board of Education, passed May 17, 2016, https://www.pps.net/cms/lib8/OR01913224/Centricity/Domain/219/FINAL%20Climate%20Change%20Reso%205.11.16%20MR%20revised.pdf.

3. Not every group we approached decided to endorse our campaign. Despite including language in the resolution, at the urging of the statewide AFL-CIO, about making students aware of "living wage jobs in the just transition away from fossil fuels," the AFL-CIO did not endorse the resolution—reflecting the tensions in a number of labor unions in the federation about joining the movement to abandon a fossil fuel–based economy.

4. "Portland School Board Bans Climate Change-Denying Materials," by Shasta Kearns Moore, *Portland Tribune*, May 19, 2016; "Portland Public Schools Ban Textbooks That Cast Doubt on Climate Change," Fox News, May 22, 2016; "Fox Hosts Upset That Portland Schools Will Stop Teaching Climate Denial to Children," Media Matters for America, May 22, 2016; "Portland Public Schools Board Bans Any Dissent from Climate Dogma," Jim Lakely, The Heartland Institute, May 22, 2016; "The Portland School Board's Climate-Change Meltdown," Editorial, *The Oregonian*, May 26, 2016; Fox News Channel—"Your World with Neil Cavuto"—Monday May 30, 2016, selected excerpts; "The Red Guards Are Green," by Cliff Kincaid, Accuracy in Media, June 6, 2016.

5. Michael Wysession, David Frank, Sophia Yancopoulos, eds., *Physical Science: Concepts in Action* (Boston: Pearson Prentice Hall, 2006).

6. Diane Hart, *History Alive!: Pursuing American Ideals*, student edition (Teachers Curriculum Inst, June 30, 2008).

Culture
Matters

Teaching Middle School Students to Advocate

Carolina Drake

Carolina Drake is a Brooklyn-based writer and reporter from Argentina who teaches Spanish to kids in New York City. Her writing has appeared in Bitch Media, Al Jazeera America, Jezebel, Hyperallergic, and independent blogs in Latin America.

ON THE LAST DAY BEFORE THE 2016 SPRING BREAK AT MANHATTAN Country School, a progressive sliding-scale tuition school in New York City, the seventh and eighth graders were busy at work with their activism campaign, "Build Bridges, Not Borders." In one classroom, a group of students gathered near the phone, waiting for their turn to call Gov. Andrew Cuomo's office to encourage the resettlement of Syrian refugees in New York. In another room, students practiced their talking points and arguments in anticipation of their lobbying trip to Washington, DC, where they would ask congressional representatives to oppose bills that would block the refugee resettlement process and sign a resolution that would condemn hateful rhetoric against Muslims in the United States.

Groups of students rotated through the various classrooms until they arrived at a mock refugee-screening process. Here, teachers pretended to be interrogators and security agents as they took the students through the nine steps asylum seekers have to go through before they even enter the United States, and explained that there are more steps after that—it takes an average of eighteen to twenty-four months to complete the process. The idea was to refute the common argument that a "terrorist" or ISIS member may come into the country disguised as a Syrian refugee, and to help the students understand what refugees who are escaping war and violence have to go through as they attempt to resettle.

This is not a standard curriculum course, but it is part of what seventh and eighth graders learn in a school committed to activism and social justice.

Each year, the seventh and eighth graders at this New York City school, where I teach Spanish, vote on a topic for their class to take on with activism. This year, a group of thirty-eight students decided to tackle Islamophobia and raise money to go to Washington, DC, to participate in the National Day of Action led by the American Immigration Lawyers Association (AILA) and lobby to let more Syrian refugees into the United States. The students searched for answers to questions, such as: What is Islamophobia? What is Islam? Is ISIS representative of Islam? How did Muslim scholars and scientists contribute to the European Renaissance? What is the experience of a Syrian person who is trying to resettle in the United States? How can we speak out against hate speech and anti-Muslim bigotry? This inquiry was a central part of the education of these thirteen- and fourteen-year-olds as they created and carried out their activism campaign.

Teaching About Reality Without Giving Up Hope

Teaching activism to middle school students matters. Years before high school and college, when the need to belong is at its strongest—young teens want to be part of something that can help them feel more powerful—that pull toward "belonging" is a source of untapped potential. "This could be done through a clique, a sports team, a rock band, or a school's activism program," Nassim Zerriffi, a seventh- and eighth-grade teacher at Manhattan Country School, told me in an email.

Knowing that we don't live in isolation and that separation is fundamental to oppression, Zerriffi tells his students that "activism is the only logical response to a thorough understanding of history."

Teaching activism allows for positive risk-taking and group identity, conveys empathy and a sense of agency, and uses ideas as instruments to solve social problems by acting on the world.

"I do encounter many skeptics," Zerriffi says. "Sometimes people initially look scornfully at children doing activism. That itself should be a sign that there's something there."

For the campaign around Syrian refugees, students learned about the complexities of history, the realities of ISIS, and why Syrians are fleeing their country. An effective activism curriculum doesn't deny these types of realities. Rather, it helps students find ways to defy reality with actions and, in the process, learn that even the smallest acts matter. Students learned that the United States announced plans to resettle at least ten thousand Syrian refugees in the next fiscal year, but that this isn't enough. After the Paris attacks of November 2015, the House of Representatives immediately passed a bill that could severely limit the acceptance of people fleeing from Syria and Iraq. Students discussed the consequences of that legislation in activism class as they depicted and critiqued the SAFE Act bill. "We'd like the representative to oppose the SAFE Act, which lengthens the process for refugees to apply for asylum. We'd also like you to oppose the Refugee Program Integrity Restoration Act (HR 4731), which gives the government the power to defund certain refugee resettlement agencies," wrote Carolina, thirteen, in one of the talking points she prepared for the class's lobbying trip to DC. "We'd also like people in Congress to speak out against Islamophobia and bigotry against Muslims and refugees . . . they already have a tough life fleeing terrorism and oppressive government," said Vidar, who is fourteen years old.

The students' activism class also examined some of the myths around refugees. For example, some politicians insist ISIS agents could sneak in with refugees, implicitly linking ISIS with the Syrian refugee crisis. Before Donald Trump clinched the Republican presidential nomination, both he and Marco Rubio agreed that the United States should turn away Syrian refugees for now, and both bandied about the possibility of closing mosques in the wake of the Paris attacks—more explicitly connecting Islamophobia to those fleeing Syria. As these current events developed, the seventh and eighth graders learned that the process to enter the United States is anything but easy. They were taken through a refugee screening and background check simulation by teachers who wanted to help them understand the refugee experience. During an assembly, a group of students in the activism committee shared what they learned with fifth and sixth graders, and also took them through the simulated screening process to help explain how improbable it would be for a "terrorist" to filter through that process.

The Muslim faith of millions of Syrian refugees has become a flashpoint in the United States, where anti-Islamic sentiment is on the rise. To learn more about Islam, students explored Islamic art and culture through museum trips and hands-on activities. The school also invited guest speakers from the Arab American Association of New York to talk about how Islamophobia affects their lives and communities, such as having NYPD spying on them. Mirna Haidar and Aber Kawas, two organizers from the association, shared their personal stories with the students about seeing negative Muslim stereotypes in the media and experiencing surveillance as part of normal life.

To raise funds for this trip, the students filmed a short video expressing why the United States should let in more refugees, how Islamophobia prevents that, and what current U.S. residents can do to help. Although the activism campaign was able to reach a broad audience and raise enough money to cover trip expenses, students also had to learn to defend their case with those who opposed their cause. The groups who met with representatives from more conservative states had to explain to them how some of their fears and reasoning were grounded in flawed beliefs. "It is incredibly difficult, if not impossible, to convince those who have illogical fears to accept more refugees," wrote Giacomo, fourteen, in his activism class reflections. "The best we can do is convince those in favor of saving lives to say so publicly and change the broken narrative we have of these innocent people."

Before the students' trip to DC, New York City lawyers who belong to the AILA explained to the class the basics of immigration law and gave talking point ideas to students, who had to write their own arguments supporting Syrian refugee resettlement and against Islamophobia as part of their homework assignments. "I was able to develop my public speaking skills as well as my ability to persuade," wrote Giacomo, who was straightforward when arguing with a Missouri representative staff member, saying, "It makes no logical sense for a terrorist to come into the U.S. through the refugee system."

"The AILA lawyers called me 'bad ass' afterwards," Giacomo added in his reflections.

Once in DC, students also met with Aisha Rahman, executive director of Karamah and head of the organization's Family Law Division, who gave the group a brief overview of the organization's work and engaged the students in a case study. She concluded by offering suggestions on how to counter some of the big misconceptions about Muslims, specifically Muslim women, circulating in the media. "At Karamah, I learned that children are forced to go to court without a lawyer, and that nine [out of] every ten [undocumented] children get deported," wrote Jessica, thirteen, in her reflections. "The case study showed me how hard it is for an undocumented person to get a visa and taught me to think about the problems undocumented people face."

Assuming Responsibility for Younger Generations

Philosopher Hannah Arendt, who describes education as "the task of renewing a common world," argued that "education is the point at which we decide whether we love the world enough to assume responsibility for it." Teaching activism is central to this task. "If other people were to take one thing from our trip to DC, it would be the difference between being activists and learning about activism," wrote Jack, thirteen, in his reflections. "Our day of lobbying was one of the first times I felt that I was having a positive impact on the world, which felt much better than brainstorming how I can convince Congress to help more Syrian refugees. If you want to make a change, do it; don't just think about it."

"Kids want to, and need to, take risks," said Zerriffi. "Talking to strangers on the street, public speaking, meeting elected officials and others in fancy offices with leather chairs, marching down the street chanting at the top of their lungs." In his teaching experience, Zerriffi says, "Just about every time, some kid is like, 'We get to do this? We're allowed to yell on the street like this?' It's exciting and feels disobedient and it's their right."

Ultimately, the experience of pushing for tangible change—loudly—makes a much deeper and more lasting impression than a textbook, Zerriffi added. "This is what democracy feels like, and it's a powerful thing for a group of young people to yell."

Getting the younger students in the school on board was also a learning process. After the DC trip, once they had grasped the issues as deeply as possible, seventh graders made their own lesson plans and were invited as guest speakers to teach activism to younger students.

"Does anyone know what Islamophobia is?" asked Osiris, thirteen, introducing the lesson to a class of fifth graders who gave him their complete attention. Two other students passed around a cartoon image with the text "Muslim Shooter = 1.3 billion people held accountable," to show how some people are more prone to be categorized as "terrorists."

Anika, who is eleven, raised her hand to say, "It's showing that all Muslims are held accountable for the actions of one person."

Interpreting another image—of a white shooter classified as a Lone Wolf with emotional issues—Gabi, eleven, said: "For the white people, it shows them like they have emotional issues or were trying to do the right thing if they shot someone, but are not as 'bad' as a black or Muslim person."

The fourth graders participated in several sessions on the foundations of Islam and the influence of Islamic culture on American music, taught by the activism coordinator. They also had seventh graders show profiles of Syrian refugees featured on the Humans of New York website. "It felt empowering to teach kids about it. Because you are passing it out to the next generation," said Osiris.

"I want you to imagine for a second every single child in the New York City school system, all 1.1 million or so," Zerriffi said. "Imagine them all walking out of school and refusing to go back until an agreed-upon set of demands are met. Think about how much potential political power there is in youth!"

Envisioning a scenario where hope is grounded in acts of defiance helps us see that no issue is truly hopeless.

Why I Teach Diverse Literature

Noah Cho

*Noah Cho teaches middle school English in the San Francisco Bay Area.
His writing has appeared on NPR's* Code Switch, Shondaland,
The Atlantic, *and* The Toast. *He spends most of his free time
going on hikes with and taking photos of his doggo, Porkchop.*

THERE ARE FEW THINGS A BIRACIAL SIXTEEN-YEAR-OLD GROWING UP IN
Southern California has in common with Nathaniel Hawthorne, author of *The Scarlet Letter.* There are even fewer experiences in the life
of that sixteen-year-old that have much if anything to do with the
events that unfold in that novel. So it's unsurprising that I have never
liked *The Scarlet Letter.*

Like many people who grew up in the American school system, I
first read Hawthorne's novel as a high school sophomore. Our English teacher led us enthusiastically through the book as I struggled to
stay awake. "You see," she said to our class, "Hawthorne keeps com-
paring little Pearl to a bird. It means that she, symbolically, wants
to . . ." [Dramatic pause.] ". . . *Fly free!*" Looking back on that class, I
often find it incredible that I became an English teacher.

Nine years after I first slogged through *The Scarlet Letter* in high
school, I found myself back at that same school, this time as a certified
teacher. I was, as most young teachers are, idealistic and filled with
grand ideas about what I could accomplish in the classroom.

In my English courses at UC Irvine, I had fallen in love with novels, stories, and writers that I could never have dreamed of back in

my high school English class. I found myself powering through Gabriel García Márquez's entire oeuvre after *Love in the Time of Cholera* appeared on my reading list for a Magical Realism course. Langston Hughes's *The Ways of White Folks* featured breathtaking prose and stories that opened my eyes to a vast world of racial dynamics far more complicated than the bubble in which I had grown up in Orange County. James Baldwin's *The Fire Next Time*, which I read with one of my most beloved college professors, inspired in me a desire for justice. Jhumpa Lahiri's *Interpreter of Maladies* spoke to me in a way that no short story collection ever had before.

But it was with Chang-Rae Lee's *Native Speaker* that my thirst for multicultural literature was fully awakened. Never before had I read a novel that so directly, powerfully, and immediately connected with my own life experience. The protagonist was a father mourning his biracial Korean son, and I was a biracial Korean son still mourning the loss of his father—to see that in a novel triggered something deep within me. I had never read a novel with a Korean protagonist, nor one that mirrored my own experience as someone caught between two cultures and trying to navigate their identity.

I always had trouble connecting with the novels I read in high school—*The Scarlet Letter*, *Pride and Prejudice*, *Heart of Darkness*—because I saw so little of myself in those works, and was in consequence less motivated to read and study them. The writing I produced in response to these books was poor as well. My English teacher constantly berated me for not caring more or trying harder; I felt like I was a terrible writer. But once I started reading works in college that spoke to me, sang to me, suddenly I couldn't *stop* writing. I fell in love with literature again.

When I was hired to teach tenth-grade English at my alma mater, I ended up replacing my own former teacher, inheriting her very classroom. Unfortunately, I also inherited the same curriculum. I was a new teacher, unproven, and felt I had to play ball. I accepted that I would not be able to change how things were done in my first year.

The first novel atop the sophomore-curriculum reading list was *The Scarlet Letter*.

There I was, a biracial teacher in Orange County with a roomful of students, 80 percent of whom were of East Asian, Southeast Asian, South Asian, and Middle Eastern descent. Not one novel written by an author of color or an LGBTQ+ author existed on the American literature curriculum. The world literature curriculum had just one: Chinua Achebe's *Things Fall Apart*. My tenth-grade Intro to Literature course could have been referred to as "Intro to White, Western Literature."

So there I was, trying to make *The Scarlet Letter* interesting to students, many of whom were actually from abroad and studying in the U.S. on student visas. We struggled through it together, but I couldn't resist taking jabs at it. I'm the type of person who finds it difficult to hide emotions, so it was with great amusement that my students watched me attempt to teach *The Scarlet Letter*. One student, one of my sharpest, said, "You totally hate this book. You should switch it out for something else."

She was right.

The next unit was a short story unit. We had one of those terrible short story collections, the ones with no discernible theme or pattern, like so many execrable textbooks in this country. But as I flipped through it, trying to find the prescribed set of stories, two in particular caught my eye. The first was Jorge Luis Borges's incredible "Book of Sand," a short story about a book with endless pages that drives its readers mad. The next story was by a writer I loved, Gabriel García Márquez, and it was one of my favorites of his: "A Very Old Man with Enormous Wings."

I decided I would teach both the Borges and García Márquez pieces, even though they weren't on the list I was supposed to be working from. The students, perhaps sensing my love for these weird and wonderful stories, responded well. Emboldened by their response, I started adding more: "TV People" by Haruki Murakami. The titular story from Lahiri's *Interpreter of Maladies*. "Home" by Langston Hughes. Parts of *Maud Martha* by Gwendolyn Brooks.

My students loved them all. For the first time, they were all genuinely engaged and interested in what we were reading. In reading these books, so many issues that I'd never discussed with students began to surface. White students also enjoyed the stories, but started realizing they had some trouble connecting with experiences of diasporas, whether African, Asian, or South American.

Since diversifying my curriculum, there is one particular conversation I've had at least once a year, up to and including this school year. The first time it happened, I was reading Gene Yang's *American Born Chinese* with my twelfth graders. One student, a white student, was discussing a scene in which the protagonist, Jin, changes his hairstyle to look more like a more popular white boy in his school.

"In this scene," my student said, "Jin is trying to become American."

I paused. "So you don't think he's American?" I asked.

"Well, no. I mean, he wants to be, but he's not."

"Even though he was born in the U.S., he's not American?"

A strange look slowly spread across his face as he realized what he'd said. "Well, I mean . . . he wants to be . . ." His voice dropped to a whisper. ". . . White?"

I don't think it even occurred to my student that his own teacher fit into the same nebulous "are you American or what?" category.

A few years later, I had been at the school long enough to change things around even more. I had been handed English classes for twelfth grade, an age I miss teaching a bit now that I'm at a middle school. It was during those years teaching twelfth graders that I developed a more multicultural set of readings. I introduced more authors from Asia, Africa, Central and South America; international films; poems and lyrics by musicians from around the world. I added a literature-to-film adaptation course, and we looked at Wong Kar Wai's *In the Mood for Love*, vaguely adapted from a short story that I had to crawl across the reaches of the Internet to find. I added a graphic novel course in which I taught Alison Bechdel's *Fun Home* and the aforementioned *American Born Chinese*.

The IB literature course I taught allowed me room to add whatever authors I wanted. The one course I couldn't touch was the AP literature course, which needed me to keep teaching "the classics" (i.e., literature mostly by straight, white, and dead men). Several of my colleagues balked at the changes I made to the other courses. Some of them lamented losing a few of the aforementioned "classics." Some of them didn't even know the depth of the diversity they *did* have in their own courses—I remember one teacher getting angry with me when I told him about speculation that Langston Hughes was gay.

There were skeptical parents, too, aware that the AP and SAT exams often favor straight white authors. Some of these parents were immigrants whose sons and daughters were finally connecting with the assigned literature. Even if they were pleased that their kids identified with these works of literature, some also feared that the knowledge of such diverse books wouldn't help them on their next standardized test.

I have, of course, had many students who do love and identify with the classics. Many of my students enjoy *Pride and Prejudice*, and I enjoyed teaching parts of *Wuthering Heights*. I'd never advocate for removing all of these novels, but I also think it's important that students of color, LGBTQ+ students, and students at other intersections see themselves in what they read. I do not want students to think they can't be writers or engaged in literature simply because they don't see themselves being portrayed in their coursework.

When I moved to the San Francisco Bay Area in 2010, I lucked into a job at an exceptionally progressive school, and I—along with two other English colleagues—have been able to develop a diverse and ever-evolving curriculum. We teach LGBTQ+ authors; we teach African American, Asian American, Latino/Latina American, and Native American and indigenous authors; we read novels and stories that deal with ableism and sexism; we look at pieces that allow us to discuss economic inequality. We try to find an "I" perspective for every single student in every one of our classes. A gender-fluid student shouldn't have to struggle to find literature they identify with. With a growing contingent of multiracial students, I also know that I need to add more books that reflect their experiences.

I talk about race and gender openly with my students, and they respond openly. They are passionate about the stories we read, always looking for connections to their own lives and experiences. As for the cis straight white students at my school, I believe it is also important for them to see me, a multiracial teacher, deeply in love with the texts I teach. It's important for them to realize that most of the books they're going to encounter in other English literature classes were written by white authors for largely white audiences, and that it's necessary to look and read beyond that.

In a way, I owe a debt to Nathaniel Hawthorne and *The Scarlet Letter*. That book, which nearly turned me against studying English back in high school, ultimately helped inspire me to change and diversity my own curriculum. For that, and for the chance to have introduced brilliant authors to the thousands of kids that have passed through my classrooms over the years, I am grateful.

Not long ago, I found myself teaching *American Born Chinese* to my seventh graders. It's a fairly quick read, so I usually assign it to be read over a weekend, and then we spend a few weeks discussing it. The students were excited to be reading a graphic novel, and they went home happy.

On Monday morning, one of my East Asian students walked into the room excitedly. He pulled his book out and showed it to me, stuffed with Post-it note annotations. He broke into a wide grin.

"This book was about my life," he said, beaming.

"I know," I said. "Mine, too."

Love for Syria:
Tackling World Crises
with Small Children

Cami Touloukian

Cami Touloukian has taught in a variety of public, private, and charter schools across the country for the past ten years. She works with future educators as a supervisor and mentor for Portland State University's Graduate School of Education.

IT WAS A TYPICAL MONDAY MORNING IN MY FIRST- AND SECOND-GRADE classroom. The students entered, greeted their friends, and chose a morning work activity. After everyone settled in, Sarat chose "Watch Me (Whip/Nae Nae)" for the cleanup song, and the students danced while cleaning before we circled up for our morning meeting. We had been learning how to greet one another in many different languages, so the students each chose a different language and said hello to their neighbors in Bengali, Japanese, Swahili, Arabic, Spanish, and other tongues. Then we moved on to sharing. The topic was simple and one of our favorites: "How are you feeling today?"

"I'm feeling nervous," said Grace, who shared that her parent was going in for surgery that morning.

"I'm happy to be at school and see my friends," exclaimed Willow, smiling brightly.

Next, it was our student teacher Ruqayya's turn. "I'm feeling sad," she said. "Is it okay if I share about it?"

The children nodded enthusiastically. I, too, was curious to hear what was concerning my friend and colleague.

"I was listening to the radio on my way to school," she said. "I am not sure if many of you know, but there is a war going on in a country that is near my home, in a place called Syria." The children's eyes grew wide and they leaned in closer. War wasn't something we had talked about in our classroom and it seemed to make them a little nervous.

"They were interviewing children who had to leave their homes because of war and were asking them how they were feeling," said Ruqayya, who identifies as a Palestinian refugee.

"One of the children was saying they wanted some paper and a crayon. Just one crayon so they could write and draw to help themselves feel better. It made me so sad and made me think about all of the things we have in our classroom that we should feel grateful for. I can't stop thinking about it."

At this point, a tear fell down Ruqayya's cheek. Willow asked Ruqayya if she would like a hug. Harper grabbed a tissue and the other kids gathered close to comfort her. I sat back in awe of this organic moment. And then, as so often happens in classrooms, it was time to transition for math. I thanked the class for taking such good care of one another and let them know we could revisit this important topic soon.

Is War "Age Appropriate"?

That evening I couldn't stop thinking about what happened during our morning meeting. Stories of the civil war in Syria, the government's crimes against humanity, against their own people, and the largest refugee crisis since World War II had been flooding my television and computer screen for months. Intellectually, I knew that the number of people affected was staggering and nearly half of them were children. Yet I had been watching in what could best be described as detached horror as I saw images of children the same age as my students being pulled from the rubble, or washing up lifeless on the beach. I had donated a small amount of money to help, but mostly felt powerless to do anything about what was happening halfway around the world.

Then there was this. This real, tangible moment that gripped my attention. After all, as a teacher, it is both my privilege and responsibility to empower children to become change makers. I knew that my students couldn't care about things they didn't know. They had shown a genuine interest in what Ruqayya shared and now I needed to figure out how to build their understanding. But I also worried that if I dug too deeply into the topic of war and refugees, parents in our mostly white, privileged community would be upset.

The following week I sat down with Ruqayya. We talked through the many concerns that had been running through my head, and ultimately agreed that this was something we shouldn't ignore. Although our students were young, they had the capacity to understand complex issues. More importantly, their hearts were wide open. So, I began by emailing parents and school administrators. It was like any other email that a teacher sends to inform families about classroom work and how they can provide support at home. Then, I sat back and waited for the inevitable pushback.

But to my surprise, most of what I got was support.

"I absolutely love that you are doing this! I trust you completely to strike the right tone," one father responded almost instantly.

Minutes later another email popped up in my inbox. "I love this idea, Cami. Thank you for not teaching down to our little ones."

It continued that way for the rest of the evening. Some parents even replied all and began to email back and forth about the importance of helping children develop global awareness and responsibility, about how this unit could build empathy, and about helping their children navigate the rampant anti-Muslim rhetoric in our country.

Planning and Pausing

The next day Ruqayya and I began fleshing out our ideas for a unit about Syria. We knew we wanted to help students build a basic understanding of the oppressive regime, the resulting civil war, and the refugee crisis. We planned to use both stories in books and real-life stories from people in our community to help students define what it means to be a refugee, and learn to push back against harmful stereotypes of people from the Middle East or the Muslim faith. Finally, we felt it was important to provide students with opportunities to learn about Syrian culture.

But our biggest goal was to build empathy that would empower students to take action. We hoped that through this unit, students would find even a small way to help. We decided to begin with a simulation the very next day.

That night, however, the resistance I initially feared became a reality. As I sat down at my laptop bubbling with excitement to do more planning, I opened an email from a parent:

> While I understand the value of cultural studies and current events, I am not sure how I feel about fielding this topic with my child. Madeline becomes overwhelmed very easily by injustice and suffering. Her heart is huge. She cries. She feels it all.

> So, I would prefer you do not bring up the concept of displaced families and refugee children in class. I know your intentions are in the right place and your language is careful, but that is my honest opinion.

I responded with some questions to help me better understand the parent's concerns, shared a bit more about our plans for the unit, and asked them to collaborate with me on differentiating how to make it work for their child.

However, I knew this mom was partially right; the issue would bring up big feelings that Madeline would need to process at home. I couldn't help but wonder though, was it so bad to feel sadness about what was happening in Syria? After all, it is sad. And perhaps tapping into our feelings is exactly what needs to happen more often at home and at school. If we don't feel anything, if we are oblivious or numb, then we won't do anything to make a difference.

I decided to wait. I wanted to see if there was a way to work with this parent to make our unit work for her and her child. I let Ruqayya know our unit was on hold and then scrambled to make alternate plans. However, a few days passed and the only thing I got was radio silence. I tried emailing and calling several times, but suddenly this parent, who was typically prompt and communicative, wasn't responding at all.

Unsure of what to do, I checked in with my assistant principal. She had been supportive from the start and gave me the green light to proceed. She encouraged me to differentiate as I saw fit, and let me know she would be there to help navigate the fallout should that parent still be upset.

Syria Simplified

Finally, we were able to begin our simulation. Our objective was to offer students a glimpse into what was happening so that they could better understand the refugee crisis. We hoped this activity would help them begin to understand that the government in Syria was unfair to its people, that the Syrian people fought back, and that this led to a civil war, which caused people to flee.

We knew we were leaving lots out. What is happening in Syria is complex. In fact, as we began planning and teaching our unit, I realized just how much I didn't know. I learned the U.S. war in Iraq contributed to the destabilization of the region, that climate change caused the worst drought in Syrian history and exacerbated tensions between the people and the government, and I began to understand the intricate role that the United States and Russia continue to play in the region. And although I chose not to teach with the same depth that I would have if working with older students, I knew we could offer students a glimpse of why people decide to flee their homes when they are faced with unfair circumstances and no good choices. As Ruqayya read aloud *Golden Domes and Silver Lanterns: A Muslim Book of Colors*, I pulled a few students aside at a time to tell them about their role.

"During this activity we will sit in a big circle. Each of you will take turns coming to a teacher to ask one question about our school day.

For example, Amir, I know you love to dance, so you could ask, 'Can we take a break to dance?' "

Amir grinned and nodded his head.

"I love to read!" Willow cheered. "Can I ask to read a book?"

"Perfect!" I answered.

I made sure they understood their job would be to approach a teacher, ask their question loud enough for all to hear, and then return to their spot in the circle. I also let them know that when they weren't asking their question, their job was to stay in the circle with the group, listen to how the teachers responded to everyone, and focus on how our answers made them feel.

After the story, we stretched and then circled up to get started. Ruqayya began by reminding them of what she had shared. As she was sharing, Madeline came to me with a concern and we stepped outside the circle to talk.

"I think you are going to be unfair and I don't want to be part of it, even if it's pretend," she said.

"Maddie, you know I wouldn't force you to do something that feels wrong inside, so if you choose not to, we can come up with a different plan for you during this time. But I have an idea. I know you love to write and draw. What if your job was a little different? How would you feel about writing and drawing about what you see? You could be the class reporter and document what is happening."

"That works for me, Cami. As long as I can sit right by you."

I told Madeline I was proud of her for advocating for herself and we rejoined the circle.

"Today we are going to do an activity that will help you understand more about the war that I told you about at morning meeting. Many of you were concerned about the children that had to leave their homes. Our activity today will help you understand why that is happening. You have each chosen a question to ask us. We will start with Clay and move our way around the circle, taking turns asking questions. Remember to pay close attention to how we answer and how our answers make you feel."

Clay approached Ruqayya first. With all of the others watching he said, "Ruqayya, can I get out a piece of paper to draw?"

Ruqayya smiled sweetly. "Of course Clay! Go ahead and get some paper. You can draw while we work."

Amir went next. He came up to me and said, "Cami, could I take a break and dance?"

"Yep! Have fun!" I replied as he danced his way back to his spot in the circle.

Next up was Harper. "Ruqayya, may I please fill up my water bottle?"

"Absolutely not!" Ruqayya said sternly. "Now back to your seat!"

The students watched with curious intrigue as some were treated with love while others were denied basic needs.

Madeline sat in the circle, too. She busily wrote speech bubbles, drew facial expressions, and jotted down notes. She was engaged and snuggled up right by my feet. I was thrilled to have adapted the activity in a way that worked for her.

We gathered after the simulation to debrief.

"Remember that we asked you to focus on how our answers made you feel. So . . . how are all of you feeling?" Ruqayya asked.

"You weren't fair!" hollered Riley.

"Why did I get to draw but Harper couldn't get a drink of water?" asked Clay. "I felt so excited because I got to do what I wanted. But when I saw how you treated Harper, I didn't feel excited anymore."

"Well, I'm just happy I got my way," said Christopher. "I mean life isn't fair anyways."

After debriefing a bit on what had happened and how everyone felt, we switched gears.

"The activity today was to help you understand the conflict in Syria and why people have decided to flee. Why do you think what happened today in our class could help you understand that?"

Willow made the connection instantaneously.

"I know!" she exclaimed. "It's because just like the things in our class today weren't fair, there are things happening in Syria that aren't fair. If I came to school every day and it was unfair like this, I would leave and go to a different school. That must be why people are leaving Syria!"

Elle chimed in next. "I wouldn't leave. No way. I would fight back.

I would go to the principal and tell on you. I would get them to help and make you treat us better."

And then, unexpectedly, Madeline jumped in. "That's it! Things in Syria are not fair and people are either choosing to leave or staying to fight back. That's why there is a war and that's why people are leaving their homes."

"Wow! You are all right on target!" Ruqayya beamed. "How many of you have heard of the word 'dictator'?"

As she explained what it means to be a dictator, Ruqayya and I guided the discussion by sharing a bit more about the regime in Syria and the protests of the Syrian people against the regime. Although we knew there are many groups involved in the Syrian war, we kept our discussion focused on the rebels and the Syrian government, the instability that their fighting caused, and the impossible decisions that the people living there had to make. As the children reflected, we led them through a whole-group discussion where they debated what they thought they would do if faced with a similar situation, and they began to understand on a simplified level what was happening halfway around the world.

Empathy

That afternoon, Ruqayya and I debriefed together and decided to proceed with a geography lesson the next day. Leo, a student in our class, had family living in Germany who had welcomed refugees from Syria into their home. He brought in maps and was excited to share where his family lived and how his family had helped.

We felt the unit was going fairly well, but that evening I was met with more resistance from Madeline's mom. This time, she was angry. She finally ended her silence and sent me an outraged email. Then she followed up with a more subdued email to the whole community:

> The Syrian refugee crisis is not a topic that I feel is age ap-
> propriate for 6- to 8-year-olds. Displacement and war are not
> teaching points I am comfortable with having my child focus on
> at school. I understand the lesson plans involve geography, art,

writing, and many other easy-to-navigate concepts, but the core issue, one that was not lost on my child, is that these are families and children fleeing their homes because of war. It caused my child anxiety, fear, and pain. These are kids. Little kids. They have many, many, many years ahead of them to contemplate the travesties of our world.

As I read her emails, those original fears about discussing Syria with children crept back into my mind. Maybe the topic of war isn't "age appropriate" after all. Just as I began to fill with self-doubt, Leo's mom responded to the group:

Thanks for starting the conversation. I definitely respect your opinion but I want to share my thoughts as well. I strongly believe that education creates empathy. As humans it is our shared experience and compassion that helps build peace. We were very proud of our family in Germany when they opened their home to refugee families. My sister-in-law needed to discuss this topic with her kids and it created a need for us to discuss it in our home as well.

War is a difficult topic, and if your child is sensitive to the issue, as hard as it is to see our kids feel pain for other people, it is also a beautiful thing that they understand the weight and gravity of what these families face. Your child will no doubt welcome a Syrian refugee with open arms and empathy if they were to join our class. That's the reason the topic is being addressed with our little kids. Because they have big hearts.

Thankfully, most of the parents in our community felt the same way and we had full support from our administrators. With fresh resolve, Ruqayya and I forged ahead. We continued to open the lines of communication with families and work with Madeline's mom in order to address her concerns. At first, we simply had to create an alternate plan for Madeline, as her mom insisted that she did not want her to be a part of this unit. However, as time passed and feelings calmed, her mom began to develop a better understanding of what we were teaching and Madeline began to join in more.

Stories and Experiences

As the unit progressed, we built on the students' initial understandings by inviting in a guest speaker named Hisham who had grown up in Syria and still had family living there. He was able to impart a sense of the oppressive regime and began by showing pictures of his family and the place he had called home.

But Hisham really captured their attention when he asked, "How many of you like to watch TV?"

Every single hand shot up.

"My favorite show is *Lego Star Wars!*" Nicholas yelled.

"Well, what would you think if I told you that the government in Syria doesn't allow *Lego Star Wars*? In fact, they don't allow any of the shows you watch. In Syria, it is illegal to watch anything other than the channels controlled by the government."

The students were shocked. They looked around wide-eyed, each asking him about their own favorite show.

Hisham had the students enthralled.

During the unit, we lined the windowsills with picture books about refugees, culture in the Middle East, and Muslim students in America. We hung Arabic artwork on the walls and used it to create our own art. We shared photos of Syrian life before the war and of children living in refugee camps afterward. We listened to Syrian music and learned Syrian dances.

One day, Ruqayya brought in a special meal to share. We invited our occupational therapist, Emily, whose family was from Syria, to join us for our meal. As students each got their own small plate of food, Emily got their attention.

"I am noticing that for our meal, everyone has their own plate. Their own food," she said.

"One of my favorite things about having a meal with my family is that it is very different from how we have a meal in America. In America, we each have our own food and our own plate. In Syrian culture, we share."

She turned to the student sitting beside her.

"Hunter, you should try some of this falafel. You will love it. It's Ruqayya's special recipe."

As Hunter accepted her offer, she continued.

"With my family, we never sit down to eat without offering to share. We all bring our special dishes and it turns into a big feast. It is one of my favorite things about my culture." And although the children only had a few dishes to try, they each turned to a friend and offered to share.

"Try this hummus! It's the best," Leo said to Amir.

"The baklava is my favorite. So sweet," Renat said to Elle. "Here, you should try some!"

Ruqayya and our visitor shared their favorite parts of their cultures, but also told students about their experiences leaving their homes and of the Islamophobia they face in the United States. The children couldn't believe it when Ruqayya shared with them about how people crossed to the other side of the street and looked at her with fear when they heard her speaking Arabic, or about her friend who was afraid to wear her hijab after she heard a Donald Trump campaign speech about Muslims.

Taking Action

The small seed that Ruqayya planted that one morning had blossomed into something beautiful. As our unit came to an end, the children asked what they could do to help. Now that they understood a little better, they wanted to give back and they wanted to make a positive impact on the world.

They wrote welcome letters to Syrian children who were coming to Oregon, and through class meetings, we decided to hold a "Love for Syria" fund-raiser for the Syrian American Medical Society. The students proudly displayed their support by making tote bags, T-shirts, love rocks, heart crayons, and banners for the fund-raiser. They even incorporated the Arabic designs and language they had learned during our unit to create artwork with affirmations of peace and love for the Syrian people. During our end of the year all-school picnic, as most of their friends played outside, ate popsicles, and soaked up the sun, our class ran our "Love for Syria" booth. When students weren't running the booth, many of them chose to invite their friends to come see what they had done and share about what they had learned. Parents even brought their own friends to share our work.

By the end of the year, my first and second graders, who began knowing nothing of the crisis in Syria, had raised nearly $800 to help.

I was also surprised by the contrast I saw between the students who had been engaged with this curriculum and those who had not.

One day, as a small group of my students decorated tablecloths for the booth, the class of first and second graders next door went rushing out for an extra recess. Oblivious, they trampled across my students' work in the mad rush to get outside.

A few even exclaimed "Cereal?! You're raising money for cereal?! That's hilarious!"

My students were crushed.

"I don't understand, Cami," Sarat said. "It's like they think it's a joke."

"They don't even care that people are hurting and dying," Riley cried, as tears streamed down his face. "I wish they knew how important this is."

"I think we should talk to them," Harper contemplated. "Maybe if we taught them some of what we have learned, they would join and help us, too. I bet they don't even know anything about Syria."

And with that, these three students went to get the kids who had trampled over their artwork. With a little love and compassion, they even convinced them to spread the word about our effort to help.

If that's not a compelling reason to engage little children with big world issues, I'm not sure what is.

Correct(ed):
Confederate Public History

James Loewen

James Loewen, professor emeritus of sociology at the University of Vermont, lives in Washington, DC, and is the award-winning author of Lies My Teacher Told Me *and* Sundown Towns, *among other works. He has won the American Book Award, the Oliver Cromwell Cox Award for Distinguished Anti-Racist Scholarship, the Spirit of America Award from the National Council for the Social Studies, and the Gustavus Myers Outstanding Book Award.*

ACROSS THE SOUTH—AND MUCH OF THE NORTH, TOO—CONFEDERATE flags, monuments, and names dot our landscape. After white supremacists held a violent rally at the Robert E. Lee statue in Charlottesville, Virginia, more people began to question these memorials and symbols. Within days, the mayor of New Orleans had taken down three Confederate statues in that city. Baltimore's mayor took down four, including one of Roger Taney, author of the infamous *Dred Scott* decision. From Helena, Montana, to Gainesville, Florida, more than twenty other Confederate monuments came down. Hundreds still stand but are getting questioned. Americans have also started questioning honors to other avowed racists, such as John C. Calhoun in Minneapolis, Orville Hubbard in Dearborn, and Edwin DeBarr at the University of Oklahoma.

These controversies offer teachable moments. Suddenly communities display new interest in U.S. history. Teachers can get students involved in researching the issues.

The main point to get across is that every monument is "a tale of two eras"—what it's about and when it went up. A monument—or historical movie, play, or novel—may say nothing accurate about the former, but it always reveals something about the latter. After students realize this, they learn twice as much when they encounter the past on the landscape, on screen, or in print.

Consider South Carolina's monument for its Gettysburg soldiers: "Abiding faith in the sacredness of states rights provided their creed here." Teachers can share with students a primary source, *The Declaration of the Immediate Causes Which Induce and Justify the Secession of South Carolina from the Federal Union*, which clearly shows that the state's leaders opposed states' rights. So the monument is flatly wrong about the 1860s.

Students who research the stone learn that it went up in 1965. At that time, South Carolina's leaders indeed believed "in the sacredness of states rights," which they used to try to stave off U.S. insistence that they desegregate their schools and let African Americans vote. So the monument has something to teach about the 1960s.

Educators *must not* present the Confederacy and the Union as moral equals. To do so is to harm historical fact. This can be hard to handle with white parents and students whose ancestors fought for the Confederacy. We must grant that many individuals fought because they were told to, friends were joining, or to protect against invasion. Many were not fighting for slavery on a personal level. Nevertheless, they were fighting for the Confederacy, whose reason for existence was slavery in the service of white supremacy.

Without educators and communities deepening their understanding of Confederate history and engaging in dialogue, we will continue to see white students abusing these symbols and creating their own examples of Confederate public history, as some did in Bloomington, Indiana, in 2016. Students countered LGBTQ students organizing rainbow flag displays of pride by coming to school the next day wearing Confederate battle flag symbols. Gay Straight Alliance (GSA) members took issue with them drawing a false equivalency between the rainbow flag and the Confederate flag, pointing out that one is a symbol of support and inclusion and the other represents a long history of racial violence and oppression. The LGBTQ students and their allies used this moment to meet with the superintendent and the hours-long meeting resulted in a policy banning the Confederate flag on campus.

If you have no local history controversies, you can get students doing local history anyway. Ask them: Who should get a historical marker in your community? Whose statue or monument deserves at least a corrective marker, if not full removal? Even when students don't actually change the landscape, they learn many skills when they actually do history like this.

Creating Inclusive Classrooms for Muslim Children

Deborah Almontaser

Deborah Almontaser, known to many as Dr. Debbie, is a community activist, advocate, entrepreneur, and educator in NYC. She is the founding principal of Khalil Gibran International Academy, a board member of the Yemeni American Merchants Association, and an advisor to the NYC Department of Education Diversity Board and Muslims for American Progress.

AS THE UNITED STATES CONTINUES TO EXPAND CULTURALLY, IT IS IM-perative that we are equipped to create inclusive classrooms that are welcoming to students of all ethnic, racial, or religious backgrounds. Every child deserves to walk into their classroom in their wholeness, free of judgment. In the current climate, it is particularly important to create inclusive classrooms and school communities for the grow-ing Muslim youth population in public schools across the country. We can show that we care about all of our students by becoming culturally and religiously literate about their customs, traditions, and rituals.

Google notwithstanding, there is no set description of a Muslim that we can turn to and say, *Aha!* this is what a Muslim is, looks like, and worships. Muslims are the most racially and ethnically diverse re-ligious group on the face of the earth. Muslims come from all seven continents, they speak different languages, eat different foods, dress differently, and have cultural practices unique to where they live. What unifies them as Muslims is their core religious belief. Today Islam is the second largest religion in the world after Christianity.

Impact of Modern Day Islamophobia

Islam and Muslims have historically been portrayed in the United States as foreign and stereotypically ridden with savagery. In the aftermath of 9/11, American Muslims faced religious prejudice and discrimination, and realized that they could no longer live as they did prior to 9/11. Muslims and those perceived to be Muslim have experienced prejudice and discrimination from the white house to the school house. For example, a 2015 report published by the Council of American-Islamic Relations revealed that 55 percent of the California Muslim students surveyed reported being subjected to some form of bullying based on their religious identity.[1] In another study done by Institute for Social Policy and Understanding, 42 percent of Muslim adults with children in K–12 school reported bullying of their children because of their faith, compared with 23 percent of Jews, 20 percent of Protestants, and 6 percent of Catholics.[2] Sadly, a teacher or administrator was reported to have been involved in one out of four bullying incidents.[3]

The Department of Justice documented between 3,000 and 5,000 hate crimes against Muslims in 2011.[4] An outgrowth of this is the Islamophobia industry, which consists of hate groups seeking to smear and malign American Muslims. Anti-Muslim attacks surged again during the 2016 election cycle, including 12 murders, 34 physical attacks, 49 verbal assaults, 49 shootings and bombings, and 56 incidents of vandalism.[5] According to the Southern Poverty Law Center, "the number of hate groups rose to 953 in 2017, from 917 in 2016."[6]

In this climate, it is critical for teachers to create a caring and nurturing classroom environment that fosters recognition, inclusion, and respect for children of all ages and all backgrounds. This includes creating curriculum that is culturally meaningful and relevant to Muslim students.

The more you know about your students, the better equipped you'll be to welcome them in the beginning of the school year. You can begin by learning about who your students are, including by asking their previous teachers, to help make your classroom accommodating and positive. Take the time to educate yourself by searching for credible sources to learn more about your students' religious and cultural backgrounds. Finding literature that is reflective of the ethnic, racial, and religious backgrounds in your classroom shows your students and their families that you value and celebrate diversity. There is nothing more powerful for students than to read about characters that look and sound like them.

In addition to surveying your students, consider surveying their parents as well. In addition to asking parents to complete a learning-style and interest survey about their child, ask parents to share with you their child's dietary needs and religious accommodations. Below are some accommodations that Muslim parents are likely to flag for you.

Dietary Accommodations

Muslims are not permitted to eat pork meat or pork by-products such as gelatin or rennet in cheese. If you decide to have a pizza party for your students, make sure you have plain or vegetable pizza options. If you want to treat your students to candy, avoid offering them Starburst and marshmallow products that are not halal or kosher certified. (Yes, Muslims can eat kosher products.) Muslims are not permitted to drink alcohol or eat products that are cooked with wine. If you're having rum cake, make sure to have an alcohol free cake option as well.

While the above is classroom-based advice, parents will also appreciate that the school cafeteria is cognizant of their child's dietary needs. The implementation of a halal-kosher menu in school is ideal. Where that is not feasible, having non-meat alternative options for students to choose from is best—peanut butter and jelly, tuna fish, and cheese sandwiches are all fine.

Physical Education Accommodations

Muslim females are known for the way they are dressed, which consists of a head scarf and modest clothing. Observant Muslim parents will bring to your attention the need for their daughter's gym clothing to be modest—loose sweat pants and a long sleeve shirt with a head covering that is suitable for sports—instead of a t-shirt and shorts. This is observed when a girl reaches puberty; however, some parents prefer modest dress for girls of all ages.

For middle and high school age girls, single-sex gym classes are preferred.

Prayer Accommodation

Muslims wash up and pray five times a day. Students are in school during the time of two of these daily prayers when daylight savings time is shorter. Therefore, having a dedicated space that is quiet and private where these children can pray for five to ten minutes daily is a very big step in terms of accommodations and one that an increasing number of middle and high schools as well as universities have been providing for Muslim students.

Some elementary schools have been providing this accommodation for 4th and 5th grade students. Like any activity in a school setting it must be supervised to ensure the safety of students; schools that have accommodated Muslim students have assigned staff to the designated prayer room.

In addition to prayer accommodations in a school setting, male students in middle and high school levels are obligated to make their Friday afternoon prayer at their local mosque. For girls the Friday afternoon prayer is optional. Parents may request permission for their child to go for Friday afternoon prayer, which is about an hour long. In urban cities, students attend neighborhood mosques. In rural areas, parents will pick up their children and bring them back to school. Schools typically request a letter from the parent and local mosque that the child is attending prayer.

Holiday Accommodations

Ramadan is a holy month for Muslims in which they refrain from eating and drinking from sunrise to sunset. During the month of Ramadan, be considerate of your Muslim students by not planning any parties or activities that involve food, to avoid making your students feel left out. During Ramadan, observant Muslims also engage in nightly prayers that can end as late as midnight. You should be aware that your middle and high school students may arrive late to class the next day.

Accommodating Muslim students during lunch time throughout Ramadan is very important. Consider arranging activities available in a separate classroom for Muslim students observing Ramadan so that they do not struggle with the temptation of food. It is also beneficial for Muslim students to have break options available to them during the day and not be pressured to perform or engage in strenuous gym classes or an overload of work. Accommodation would include not penalizing them for lack of energy in the classroom or for arriving a few minutes late to class. If Ramadan falls during the end of the school year, consider proctoring state tests in the evening, after students break their fast. A number of school districts have accommodated middle and high school students in these ways.

Some Muslim students are exempt from fasting for health reasons but may wish to avoid unwanted attention. Middle and high school girls, for example, are exempt from fasting during their menstrual cycle to ensure they are getting enough fluids and nourishment (they can resume fasting at a later time to make up the days missed). Teachers and school personnel should not make it obvious to other students or question a student who is not fasting.

In addition to Ramadan, Muslims around the world observe two other holidays or Eids. The first Eid is right after Ramadan. The second Eid is two months and 10 days after Ramadan. Both Eids are observed with morning prayers at the mosque followed by family festivities. Muslim students will be absent during these two holidays; therefore it would be beneficial to avoid giving a test on such dates (in cities with large Muslim population, the two Eids are official holidays). As with all holidays, use the two Eids as teachable moments to introduce your non-Muslim students to Islamic culture and traditions.

Student Voice

It is imperative that educators provide an environment where students feel free, confident, and unembarrassed about their identity. In light of the country's growing Islamophobia, many students, consciously or subconsciously, feel targeted and excluded. Educators must make special efforts to empower Muslim students to have a voice and a place at the table along with other students. Through a supportive and inclusive environment, Muslim students will be motivated to participate in school activities.

Giving students voice is an important aspect of the teaching profession; we want students to share their thoughts and feelings, as well as represent when they want to. But this must be accomplished in a thoughtful way; one caution for us as educators is to make sure we never put a student in the position of needing to represent their community. Time after time, I have seen or heard about Muslim students being put in the position of speaking on behalf of 1.6 billion Muslims. Our students should not be seen as experts to represent Islam or Muslims or the events of 9/11. Few things feel worse for Muslim students than for the lesson to turn to the events of 9/11, and for all heads, including the teacher's, to turn towards them.

Parent, Community, and School Partnership

Another way to meet the needs of your Muslim students is to connect with their families. Many parents will welcome the opportunity to come in and present about their culture, bring in cultural artifacts, food, and clothing. Parents can also be a good source for supplemental materials, projects, and activities for your students. When parents are welcomed by teachers and administrators, they are more likely to get involved in their children's school. Their presence will motivate their children to do well in school. A parent who feels a part of the school "family" is more likely to play an active role whether it be participating in the PTA, learning English, or being involved and concerned about their child's academic performance.

A good start is for principals and teachers to simply greet parents when they bring their children to school. When greeting Muslim parents, wait to see how they will greet you. Observant Muslims do not engage in physical contact with the opposite sex. Some may shake hands, but wait for their cue to avoid making them feel awkward. Being culturally responsive to parents will promote a good relationship among parents and school staff.

In addition to parents, local mosques are a good source of support for Muslim students. Representatives from Muslim-based nonprofits and university centers specializing on Islam and Muslims would be happy to come present in schools and to offer any assistance needed to understand and respect Muslim students and make them feel welcome and valued in school settings.

A Brief Overview of Muslims in the U.S.

Today, the U.S. has one of the most thriving Muslim communities in the West. The latest Pew numbers from 2017 show the country is home to an estimated 3.45 million Muslims of all ages—about 1.1 percent of the total U.S. population—while other sources indicate that there are as many as 8 to 12 million Muslims nationally. By 2050, Pew researchers estimate Islam will supplant Judaism as the second-most popular religion in the U.S. with 8.1 million Muslims ultimately making up 2.1 percent of the future population.

As with other religions, adherents to Islam come from a variety of faith traditions and denominations. Sunni Muslims are widely recognized as the largest sect, comprising approximately 90 percent of Muslims worldwide. The second largest group identifies as Shia. Sunnis, Shias, and other Muslim-faith traditions share certain core beliefs, and each community has practices and beliefs that may be unique.

The American Muslim community is very diverse, ranging from over eighty countries.[7] Within the American Muslim community, the three largest groups are African Americans, who constitute the largest group, followed by South Asians from the Far East, and Arabs from the twenty-two Arab League nations, with a growing number of Caucasian and Latino American Muslims as well.

Notes

1. Fatima Dadabhoy, "Mislabeled: The Impact of School Bullying and Discrimination on California Muslim Students," Council of American-Islamic Relations, California, 2015, https://ca.cair.com/sfba/wp-content/uploads/sites/10/2018/04/CAIR-CA-2015-Bullying-Report-Web.pdf.

2. Dalia Mogahed and Youssef Chouhoud, "American Muslim Poll 2017: Muslims at the Crossroads," Institute for Social Policy and Understanding, 2017,

https://www.ispu.org/wp-content/uploads/2017/03/American-Muslim-Poll -2017-Report.pdf.

3. Mogahed and Chouhoud, "American Muslim Poll 2017."

4. Booth Gunter et al., "FBI: Bias Crimes Against Muslims Remain at High Levels," *The Intelligence Report*, February 2013, Southern Poverty Law Center, https://www.splcenter.org/fighting-hate/intelligence-report/2013/fbi-bias -crimes-against-muslims-remain-high-levels.

5. Bridge Initiative Team, "When Islamophobia Turns Violent: The 2016 U.S. Presidential Elections," Georgetown University Bridge Initiative, 2018, https://bridge.georgetown.edu/research/islamophobia-turns-violent.

6. Southern Poverty Law Center, "Hate Groups Reach Record High," February 19, 2019, https://www.splcenter.org/news/2019/02/19/hate-groups -reach-record-high.

7. Center for Muslim-Christian Understanding, "Project MAPS: Muslims in the American Public Square," Georgetown University School of Foreign Service, 2001.

Appendix: Books on Immigration for Young Readers

This list was compiled by Jay Fung, the librarian at Manhattan Country School in New York City.

Young children (ages 4–7)

Pancho Rabbit and the Coyote by Duncan Tonatiuh
Mustafa by Marie-Louise Gay
Grandfather's Journey by Allen Say
This Is Our House by Hyewon Yum
The Keeping Quilt by Patricia Polacco
Dreamers by Yuyi Morales
Carmela Full of Wishes by Matt De La Peña
Landed by Yangsook Choi
Marwan's Journey by Patricia de Arias
Before I Leave by Jessixa Bagley
The Name Jar by Yangsook Choi
Teacup by Rebecca Young
Where Will I Live? by Rosemary McCarney
Two White Rabbits by Jairo Buitrago
Stepping Stones: A Refugee Family's Journey by Margriet Ruurs
Four Feet, Two Sandals by Karen Lynn Williams

Middle grades (ages 8–11)

The Day War Came by Nicola Davies
A Different Pond by Bao Phi
Inside Out and Back Again by Thanhha Lai
Azzi in Between by Sarah Garland
A Long Walk to Water by Linda Sue Park
How Tía Lola Came to Stay by Julia Alvarez
Somos Como Las Nubes/We Are Like the Clouds by Jorge Argueta
Downtown Boy by Juan Felipe Herrera
It Ain't So Awful, Falafel by Firoozeh Dumas
Undocumented by Duncan Tonatiuh
The Only Road by Alexandra Diaz
Nowhere Boy by Katherine Marsh
My Family Divided by Diane Guerrero
The Red Pencil by Andrea Davis Pinkney
The Dragon's Child by Laurence Yep

Pre-teens and teens (ages 12–16 and up)

The Distance Between Us by Reyna Grande
Shooting Kabul by N.H. Senzai
A Time of Miracles by Anne-Laure Bondoux
Esperanza Rising by Pam Muñoz Ryan
Americanized: Rebel Without a Green Card by Sara Saedi
The Arrival by Shaun Tan
The Radius of Us by Marie Marquardt
Voces Sin Fronteras foreword by Meg Medina
Enrique's Journey by Sonia Nazario
Illegal by Eoin Colfer
The Circuit: Stories from the Life of a Migrant Child by Francisco Jiménez
I Lived on Butterfly Hill by Marjorie Agosin
Their Great Gift: Courage, Sacrifice and Hope in a New Land by John Coy
Something in Between by Melissa De La Cruz
The Sun Is Also a Star by Nicola Yoon

Permissions

To the extent a separate copyright attaches to *Teaching When the World Is on Fire* as a collective work, The New Press is the copyright owner of any such copyright on the anthology as a collective work. Below are the permissions granted for use of respective individual pieces.

"I Shall Create!" © 2019 William Ayers. All rights reserved. In this essay, lines from the poem "Paul Robeson" by Gwendolyn Brooks, originally published in *Family Pictures*, Detroit: Broadside Press, 1971, are reprinted by permission of Brooks Permissions.

"Teaching Politics in the Age of Trump" © 2019 Justin Christensen for *PBS News Hour*. All rights reserved. Reprinted by permission of the author.

"The Three Illusions" © 2019 Julia Putnam. All rights reserved.

"Standing Up Against Hate" © 2019 Mica Pollock for *Teaching Tolerance*. All rights reserved. Reprinted by permission of the author.

"Yes, Race and Politics Belong in the Classroom" © 2019 H. Richard Milner IV for *Education Week*. All rights reserved. Reprinted by permission of the author.

"Cops or Counselors?" © 2019 Pedro A. Noguera. All rights reserved.

"How Hurricane Harvey Altered My Perspective as a Teacher" © 2019 Jeff Collier for *Education Week*. All rights reserved. Reprinted by permission of the author.

"I Was Raised to Believe Education Could Keep Me Safe," previously published as "A Lesson on Jordan Edwards" © 2019 fredrick scott salyers for *Chalkbeat*/The Marshall Project. All rights reserved. Reprinted by permission of the author.

"Calling on Omar" © 2019 Carla Shalaby. All rights reserved.

"School Justice" © 2019 T. Elijah Hawkes. All rights reserved.

"Don't Say Nothing" © 2019 Jamilah Pitts for *Teaching Tolerance*. All rights reserved. Reprinted by permission of the author.

"Black Teachers, Black Youth, and Reality Pedagogy" © 2019 Christopher Emdin. All rights reserved.

"How One Elementary School Sparked a Citywide Movement to Make Black Students' Lives Matter" © 2019 Wayne Au and Jesse Hagopian for *Rethinking Schools*. All rights reserved. Reprinted by permission of the author and *Rethinking Schools*.

"The Fire" © 2019 Sarah Ishmael and Jonathan Tunstall. All rights reserved.

"Engaging and Embracing Black Parents" © 2019 Allyson Criner Brown. All rights reserved.

"Who Do I Belong To?" © 2019 Natalie Labossiere for *Rethinking Schools*. All rights reserved. Reprinted by permission of the author and *Rethinking Schools*.

"To My Sons' Future Teacher, Colleague, Sister/Brother, Co-madre, Maestra, Comrade, Friend" © 2019 Crystal T. Laura. All rights reserved.

"Sexual Harassment and the Collateral Beauty of Resistance, previously published as "What Students Are Capable Of: Sexual Harassment and the Collateral Beauty of Resistance" © 2019 Camila Arze

Torres Goitia for *Rethinking Schools*. All rights reserved. Reprinted by permission of the author and *Rethinking Schools*.

"Believe Me the First Time" © 2019 Dale Weiss for *Rethinking Schools*. All rights reserved. Reprinted by permission of the author and *Rethinking Schools*.

"Nothing About Us, Without Us, Is for Us" © 2019 Maya Lindberg for *Teaching Tolerance*. All rights reserved. Reprinted by permission of the author.

"Climate Science Meets a Stubborn Obstacle: Students" © 2019 Amy Harmon for *The New York Times*. All rights reserved. Reprinted by permission of the author and *The New York Times*.

"Teachers vs. Climate Change" © 2019 Bill Bigelow. All rights reserved.

"Teaching Middle School Students to Advocate," previously published as "Lessons in Activism: Middle School Students Advocate for Syrian Refugees" © 2016 Carolina Drake for *Truthout*. All rights reserved. Reprinted by permission of the author.

"Why I Teach Diverse Literature" © 2019 Noah Cho for *The Toast*. All rights reserved. Reprinted by permission of the author.

"Love for Syria" © 2019 Cami Touloukian for *Rethinking Schools*. All rights reserved. Reprinted by permission of the author and *Rethinking Schools*.

"Correct(ed): Confederate Public History," previously published as "Confederate Public History" © 2019 James Loewen for *National Education Association*. All rights reserved. Reprinted by permission of the author.

"Creating Inclusive Classrooms for Muslim Children" © 2019 Deborah Almontaser. All rights reserved.

About Rethinking Schools

Some of the articles in this book first appeared in *Rethinking Schools* magazine. Rethinking Schools is a nonprofit publisher and advocacy organization dedicated to sustaining and strengthening public education through social justice teaching and education activism. Visit www.rethinkingschools.org to subscribe to *Rethinking Schools* magazine and to see Rethinking Schools books.

About the Editor

MacArthur Award winner **Lisa Delpit** is the Felton G. Clark Professor of Education at Southern University and A&M College. The author of *Other People's Children* and *"Multiplication Is for White People"* and the co-editor, with Joanne Kilgour Dowdy, of *The Skin That We Speak* (all published by The New Press), she lives in Baton Rouge, Louisiana.

Publishing in the Public Interest

Thank you for reading this book published by The New Press. The New Press is a nonprofit, public interest publisher. New Press books and authors play a crucial role in sparking conversations about the key political and social issues of our day.

We hope you enjoyed this book and that you will stay in touch with The New Press. Here are a few ways to stay up to date with our books, events, and the issues we cover:

- Sign up at www.thenewpress.com/subscribe to receive updates on New Press authors and issues and to be notified about local events
- Like us on Facebook: www.facebook.com/newpress books
- Follow us on Twitter: www.twitter.com/thenewpress

Please consider buying New Press books for yourself; for friends and family; or to donate to schools, libraries, community centers, prison libraries, and other organizations involved with the issues our authors write about.

The New Press is a 501(c)(3) nonprofit organization. You can also support our work with a tax-deductible gift by visiting www.thenewpress.com/donate.

Printed in the USA
CPSIA information can be obtained
at www.ICGtesting.com
JSHW022217140824
68134JS00018B/1113